SPECTRUM®

Test Prep

Grade 1

Published by Spectrum®
an imprint of Carson-Dellosa Publishing LLC
Greensboro, NC

Visit *carsondellosa.com* for correlations to Common Core State, national, and Canadian provincial standards.

Spectrum®
An imprint of Carson-Dellosa Publishing LLC
P.O. Box 35665
Greensboro, NC 27425 USA

ISBN 978-0-7696-8121-4

10-266137784

Table of Contents

What's Inside?

This workbook is designed to help you and your first grader understand what he or she will be expected to know on standardized tests.

Practice Pages

The workbook is divided into two sections: English Language Arts and Mathematics. The practice activities in this workbook provide students with practice in each of these areas. Each section has practice activities that have questions similar to those that will appear on the standardized tests. Students should use a pencil to fill in the correct answers and to complete any writing on these activities. If needed, passages may be read aloud to the student.

National Standards

Before each practice section is a list of the national standards covered by that section. These standards list the knowledge and skills that students are expected to master at each grade level. The shaded *What it means* sections will help to explain any information in the standards that might be unfamiliar.

Mini-Tests and Final Tests

When your student finishes the practice pages for specific standards, your student can move on to a mini-test that covers the material presented on those practice activities. After an entire set of standards and accompanying practice pages are completed, your student should take the final tests, which incorporate materials from all the practice pages in that section.

Final Test Answer Sheet

The final tests have a separate answer sheet that mimics the style of the answer sheets the students will use on the standardized tests. The answer sheets appear at the end of each final test.

How Am I Doing?

The *How Am I Doing?* pages are designed to help students identify areas where they are proficient and areas where they still need more practice. They will pinpoint areas where more work is needed as well as areas where your student excels. Students can keep track of each of their mini-test scores on these pages.

Answer Key

Answers to all the practice pages, mini-tests, and final tests are listed by page number and appear at the end of the book.

To find a complete listing of the national standards in each subject area, you can access the following Web sites:

The National Council of Teachers of English: www.ncte.org
National Council of Teachers of Mathematics: www.nctm.org/standards

English Language Arts Standards

Standard 1 *(See pages 7–10.)*
Students read a wide range of print and nonprint texts to build an understanding of texts, of themselves, and of the cultures of the United States and the world; to acquire new information; to respond to the needs and demands of society and the workplace; and for personal fulfillment. Among these texts are fiction and nonfiction, classic and contemporary works.

Standard 2 *(See pages 7–11.)*
Students read a wide range of literature from many periods in many genres to build an understanding of the many dimensions (e.g., philosophical, ethical, aesthetic) of human experience.

Standard 3 *(See pages 11–19.)*
Students apply a wide range of strategies to comprehend, interpret, evaluate, and appreciate texts. They draw on their prior experience, their interactions with other readers and writers, their knowledge of word meaning and of other texts, their word identification strategies, and their understanding of textual features (e.g., sound-letter correspondence, sentence structure, context, graphics).

What it means:
- Students draw on a wide array of clues while they are reading to comprehend and make connections. Some of these strategies may include: recognizing story characteristics; distinguishing fact from opinion; making inferences to guide predictions; determining the meaning of unknown words based on context; and interpreting information from pictures, diagrams, charts, or graphic organizers.

Standard 4 *(See pages 22–29.)*
Students adjust their use of spoken, written, and visual language (e.g., conventions, style, vocabulary) to communicate effectively with a variety of audiences and for different purposes.

Standard 5 *(See pages 28–32.)*
Students employ a wide range of strategies as they write and use different writing process elements appropriately to communicate with different audiences for a variety of purposes.

Standard 6 *(See pages 33–38.)*
Students apply knowledge of language structure, language conventions (e.g., spelling and punctuation), media techniques, figurative language, and genre to create, critique, and discuss print and nonprint texts.

Standard 7 *(See page 41.)*
Students conduct research on issues and interests by generating ideas and questions, and by posing problems. They gather, evaluate, and synthesize data from a variety of sources (e.g., print and nonprint texts, artifacts, people) to communicate their discoveries in ways that suit their purpose and audience.

Standard 8 *(See pages 42–43.)*
Students use a variety of technological and informational resources (e.g., libraries, databases, computer networks, video) to gather and synthesize information and to create and communicate knowledge.

English Language Arts Standards

Standard 9 *(See page 45.)*
Students develop an understanding of and respect for diversity in language use, patterns, and dialects across cultures, ethnic groups, geographic regions, and social roles.

What it means:
- A *dialect* is a regional variation in vocabulary, grammar, and pronunciation within a single language used by members of a group. Social roles and ethnic groups can be identified by use of specific dialects.

Standard 10
Students whose first language is not English make use of their first language to develop competency in the English language arts and to develop understanding of content across the curriculum.

Standard 11 *(See page 46.)*
Students participate as knowledgeable, reflective, creative, and critical members of a variety of literacy communities.

What it means:
- Young children learn language quickly through meaningful interactions with caring adults. Children learn and better comprehend text when they have opportunities to bring their experiences with life and other texts to reading experiences.

Standard 12 *(See page 47.)*
Students use spoken, written, and visual language to accomplish their own purposes (e.g., for learning, enjoyment, persuasion, and the exchange of information).

Name _____   Date _____

English Language Arts

Understanding Fiction
Reading and Comprehension

DIRECTIONS: Read the story. Choose the best answer to each question about the story. Practice with the example.

Example:

The boy ran fast. He did not want to be late. Mom was making chicken. It was his favorite food.

What was Mom making?

(A) shoes   (C) puddles

(B) chicken   (D) tacos

Answer: (B)

 Clue   Carefully read the whole story.

Steve and his sister were playing. They were in the yard. A bird landed on the fence.

They watched the bird fly to the ground. It picked up some grass. Then, it flew to a tree. Steve said the bird was making a nest.

1. Who was with Steve?

(A) Steve's mother

(B) Steve's sister

(C) Steve's dog

(D) Steve's friend

2. Where did the bird land?

(F) on the fence

(G) on the roof

(H) under the tree

(J) on Steve

3. What does Steve say the bird is doing?

(A) looking for food

(B) playing

(C) watching them play in the yard

(D) building a nest

4. Where does this story take place?

(F) in Steve's yard

(G) at school

(H) at a park

(J) at the zoo

GO

DIRECTIONS: Read the story. Choose the best answer to each question about the story.

Get Warm

Brenda Butterfly was cold. She did not like it. She liked the sunny, warm weather. But it was fall. "What can I do to get warm?"

Her friend Buddy knew what to do. "I think you should follow the birds. They fly to warm places in winter."

Brenda liked the idea. "That sounds great! Will you come with me, Buddy?"

They followed a flock of birds. It was a long trip. But it was so warm and sunny! Brenda and Buddy smiled. What a good idea!

There were many butterflies in this place. The flowers were colorful. Maybe Brenda and Buddy would stay.

5. Brenda did not like _____ .

   (A) sunny weather

   (B) being cold

   (C) her friend Buddy

   (D) birds

6. What did Buddy think Brenda should do?

   (F) nothing

   (G) light a fire

   (H) get new coats

   (J) follow the birds

7. Why should she follow the birds?

   (A) to find water

   (B) to see snow

   (C) to get to a warm place

   (D) to get to a cold place

8. Two things Brenda and Buddy liked now were _____ .

   (F) their bird friends and fish

   (G) colorful flowers and being warm

   (H) flying far and the moon

   (J) cold air and gray skies

STOP

Name _____ Date _____

Understanding Nonfiction
Reading and Comprehension

DIRECTIONS: Read the story. Choose the best answer to each question about the story.

Spiders

Spiders are animals. All spiders have eight legs. Most spiders spin webs of silk. The webs help the spiders catch food. They eat mostly insects.

Some spiders are big. There is one as big as a man's hand. Other spiders are very small. One spider is as small as the tip of a pin.

1. Spiders are _____ .

- (A) insects
- (B) animals
- (C) plants
- (D) people

2. Spider webs are made of _____ .

- (F) silk
- (G) rope
- (H) wire
- (J) metal

3. Why do spiders spin webs?

- (A) for fun
- (B) to build a nest
- (C) to plant flowers
- (D) to catch food

4. Why was this story written?

- (F) to tell about spiders
- (G) to tell about insects
- (H) to scare you
- (J) to make you giggle

GO

Name _____   Date _____

DIRECTIONS: Read the story. Choose the best answer to each question about the story.

Apples

Apples need all four seasons to grow. In the spring, apple trees grow white flowers and small green leaves first. Then, the flowers drop off. Tiny green apples start to grow as the weather gets warm.

In the summer, the tree branches fill with small apples. In the fall, the big apples are ready to be picked. Leaves start to drop off the branches.

In the winter, the apple tree will rest. It does not grow any leaves or apples. It is getting ready to grow flowers and apples again in the spring.

5. **What grows on the apple tree branches first?**
   - (A) apples
   - (B) beehives
   - (C) flowers and leaves
   - (D) small animals

6. **In what season do the apples grow the most?**
   - (F) fall
   - (G) summer
   - (H) winter
   - (J) spring

7. **What happens to apple trees in the winter?**
   - (A) They rest.
   - (B) They grow very tall.
   - (C) Farmers cut them down.
   - (D) They grow apples.

8. **Why was this story written?**
   - (F) to tell about winter
   - (G) to tell about farming
   - (H) to tell about flowers
   - (J) to tell about apples

STOP

Name _____ Date _____

Sentence Comprehension
Reading and Comprehension

DIRECTIONS: Read the sentence. Choose the picture that completes or matches the sentence. Practice with the examples.

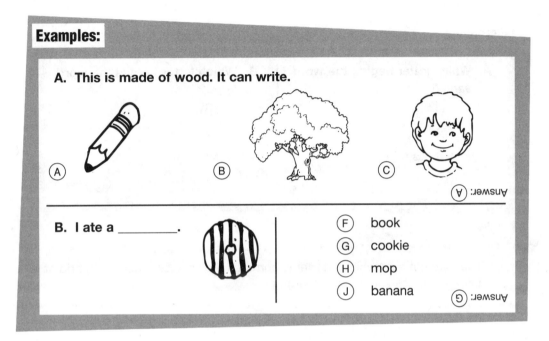

Examples:

A. This is made of wood. It can write.

(A)   (B)   (C)

Answer: (A)

B. I ate a _____.

- (F) book
- (G) cookie
- (H) mop
- (J) banana

Answer: (G)

1. This is hot. It helps things grow.

(A)   (B)   (C)

2. You smell with this. It is on your face.

(F)   (G)   (H)

3. This is my _____.

- (A) dog
- (B) school
- (C) lake
- (D) friend

4. There is a _____ in front of the school.

- (F) bike
- (G) frog
- (H) flag
- (J) boy

STOP

English Language Arts

| 3.0 |

Letter Recognition
Reading and Comprehension

DIRECTIONS: Look at the word in italics. Choose the letter that begins the word. Example A is done for you. Practice with example B.

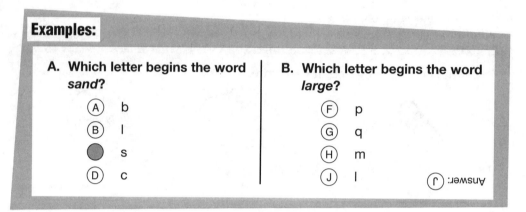

Examples:

A. Which letter begins the word *sand*?

(A) b
(B) l
(●) s
(D) c

B. Which letter begins the word *large*?

(F) p
(G) q
(H) m
(J) l

Answer: (J)

 Clue If you are not sure which answer is correct, take your best guess. Get rid of answer choices you know are wrong.

---

1. **Which letter begins the word *park*?**

(A) v
(B) w
(C) b
(D) p

2. **Which letter begins the word *dog*?**

(F) d
(G) b
(H) y
(J) o

3. **Which letter begins the word *nice*?**

(A) s
(B) n
(C) u
(D) k

4. **Which letter begins the word *talk*?**

(F) j
(G) f
(H) t
(J) l

STOP

Name _____ Date _____

3.0

Word Recognition
Reading and Comprehension

DIRECTIONS: Read the word. Look at the underlined part. Then, read the word choices. Look for the word with the same sound as the underlined part and mark it. Practice with the examples.

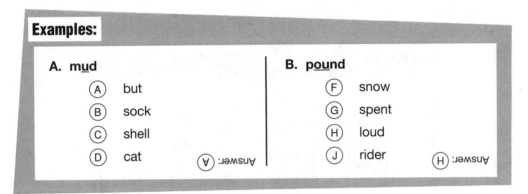

Examples:

A. mud
- (A) but
- (B) sock
- (C) shell
- (D) cat

Answer: (A)

B. pound
- (F) snow
- (G) spent
- (H) loud
- (J) rider

Answer: (H)

Clue Say each word out loud. Listen for the sound of the underlined part.

1. rose
- (A) rule
- (B) bake
- (C) pony
- (D) nine

2. spoon
- (F) here
- (G) smooth
- (H) after
- (J) chip

3. peach
- (A) quiet
- (B) push
- (C) last
- (D) need

4. ride
- (F) miss
- (G) line
- (H) street
- (J) horse

STOP

English Language Arts

3.0

Identifying
Beginning Sounds
Reading and Comprehension

DIRECTIONS: Look at the picture. Read the word above the picture. Then, read the words beside the picture. Choose the word with the same beginning sound as the picture. Practice with the example.

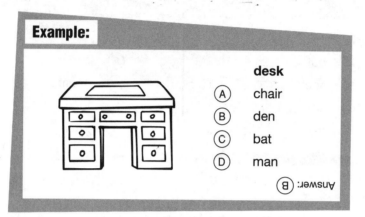

Example:

desk

- (A) chair
- (B) den
- (C) bat
- (D) man

Answer: (B)

Clue — Say the name of the picture to yourself. Listen closely to the word choices.

1. rabbit

- (A) man
- (B) bike
- (C) paper
- (D) ring

2. mop

- (F) miss
- (G) hill
- (H) clock
- (J) win

3. bag

- (A) vase
- (B) top
- (C) bell
- (D) fish

4. tie

- (F) pin
- (G) girl
- (H) shell
- (J) tag

STOP

English Language Arts

3.0

Identifying Ending Sounds
Reading and Comprehension

DIRECTIONS: Read each word. Choose the word with the same ending sound as the first word. Practice with the examples.

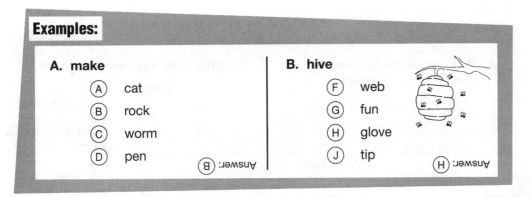

Examples:

A. make
- (A) cat
- (B) rock
- (C) worm
- (D) pen

Answer: (B)

B. hive
- (F) web
- (G) fun
- (H) glove
- (J) tip

Answer: (H)

Clue Listen carefully to the ending sound of each word.

1. star
- (A) mop
- (B) leaf
- (C) jar
- (D) five

2. leg
- (F) rug
- (G) gone
- (H) rich
- (J) grab

3. stew
- (A) net
- (B) wheel
- (C) barn
- (D) new

4. hit
- (F) dish
- (G) win
- (H) not
- (J) hear

5. bell
- (A) rest
- (B) hill
- (C) boat
- (D) cab

6. fan
- (F) ten
- (G) bird
- (H) saw
- (J) hand

STOP

English Language Arts

| 3.0 |

Vowel Sounds and Rhyming Words
Reading and Comprehension

DIRECTIONS: Read the question and say the name of the picture. Then, read the word choices. Choose the best answer. Example A is done for you. Practice with example B.

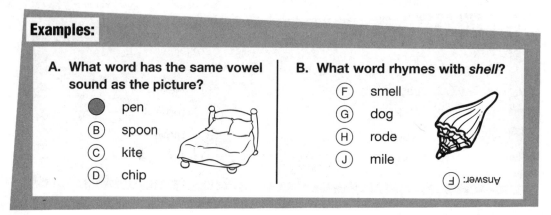

Examples:

A. **What word has the same vowel sound as the picture?**

- ⬤ pen
- Ⓑ spoon
- Ⓒ kite
- Ⓓ chip

B. **What word rhymes with *shell*?**

- Ⓕ smell
- Ⓖ dog
- Ⓗ rode
- Ⓙ mile

Answer: (F)

 Clue   Read all the choices before you mark your answer.

1. **Which word has the same vowel sound as the picture?**

   - Ⓐ mouse
   - Ⓑ long
   - Ⓒ tick
   - Ⓓ spoon

2. **Which word has the same vowel sound as the picture?**

   - Ⓕ bead
   - Ⓖ hive
   - Ⓗ quilt
   - Ⓙ apple

3. **Which word has the same vowel sound as *might*?**

   - Ⓐ pin
   - Ⓑ time
   - Ⓒ from
   - Ⓓ soul

4. **Which word rhymes with *tough*?**

   - Ⓕ crow
   - Ⓖ pool
   - Ⓗ puff
   - Ⓙ ton

STOP

English Language Arts

3.0

Compound Words and Sentence Structure
Reading and Comprehension

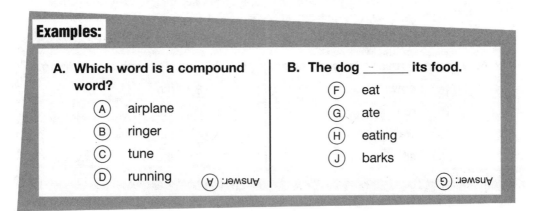

Examples:

A. Which word is a compound word?

- (A) airplane
- (B) ringer
- (C) tune
- (D) running

Answer: (A)

B. The dog _____ its food.

- (F) eat
- (G) ate
- (H) eating
- (J) barks

Answer: (G)

Clue A **compound word** is made when two words are put together to make a new word.

DIRECTIONS: Read the words. Choose the word that is a compound word.

1.
- (A) toolbox
- (B) kitchen
- (C) gate
- (D) walked

2.
- (F) warning
- (G) flowerpot
- (H) glasses
- (J) children

3.
- (A) jumping
- (B) pencil
- (C) teacup
- (D) rushed

4.
- (F) find
- (G) lady bug
- (H) sledding
- (J) really

DIRECTIONS: Read the sentence and the word choices. One word will fill in the blank. Mark your choice.

5. I am _____ a new bike.
- (A) gets
- (C) got
- (B) get
- (D) getting

6. I am _____ than you.
- (F) bigger
- (H) biggest
- (G) big
- (J) blue

7. I _____ books.
- (A) readed
- (C) read
- (B) reads
- (D) reading

8. He _____ hot.
- (F) weren't
- (H) won't
- (G) can't
- (J) wasn't

STOP

English Language Arts

| 3.0 |

Identifying Word Meanings
Reading and Comprehension

DIRECTIONS: Read each phrase and the word choices. Choose the word that matches the phrase.

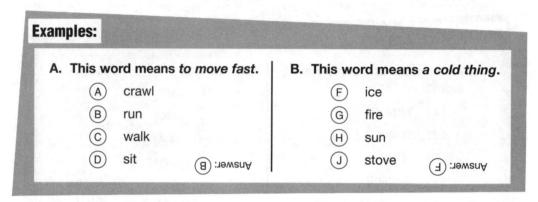

Examples:

A. This word means *to move fast*.

- Ⓐ crawl
- Ⓑ run
- Ⓒ walk
- Ⓓ sit

Answer: (B)

B. This word means *a cold thing*.

- Ⓕ ice
- Ⓖ fire
- Ⓗ sun
- Ⓙ stove

Answer: (F)

1. This word means *a thing that flies*.

- Ⓐ pen
- Ⓑ book
- Ⓒ bird
- Ⓓ cup

2. This word means *a thing that birds build*.

- Ⓕ chair
- Ⓖ girl
- Ⓗ nest
- Ⓙ paper

3. This word means *to drink a little*.

- Ⓐ spill
- Ⓑ tip
- Ⓒ sip
- Ⓓ toss

4. This word means *to stay on top of water*.

- Ⓕ float
- Ⓖ sink
- Ⓗ pin
- Ⓙ zip

5. This word means *the noise a dog makes*.

- Ⓐ bark
- Ⓑ purr
- Ⓒ cut
- Ⓓ land

6. This word means *a kind of fruit*.

- Ⓕ wood
- Ⓖ cart
- Ⓗ apple
- Ⓙ bed

STOP

English Language Arts

| 3.0 |

Using Context Clues
Reading and Comprehension

DIRECTIONS: Read the sentence and word choices. Choose the word that best completes the sentence.

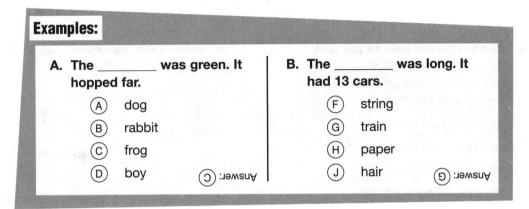

Examples:

A. The _____ was green. It hopped far.
- (A) dog
- (B) rabbit
- (C) frog
- (D) boy

Answer: (C)

B. The _____ was long. It had 13 cars.
- (F) string
- (G) train
- (H) paper
- (J) hair

Answer: (G)

Clue

Make sure you read all of the choices. When you think you see the correct answer, put your finger next to it.

1. Sam sat in the _____ . He soon fell asleep.
- (A) ice
- (B) chair
- (C) hammer
- (D) nail

2. The bee flew to its _____ . It went inside.
- (F) corner
- (G) cup
- (H) hive
- (J) honey

3. There are four _____ on the shelf. Tuti read them all.
- (A) cats
- (B) animals
- (C) suns
- (D) books

4. The joke was _____ . We all smiled.
- (F) funny
- (G) sad
- (H) blue
- (J) bread

STOP

English Language Arts

| 1.0–3.0 |

For pages 7–19

Mini-Test 1

Reading and Comprehension

DIRECTIONS: Read each story. Then, answer each question.

1. **Emma wanted to ride her bike to the park. She asked Matt to go, too. Mike could not ride with her. His bike had a flat tire. What was wrong with Matt's bike?**

   (A) Emma rode her bike.

   (B) Emma went to the park.

   (C) His bike had a flat tire.

   (D) Matt does not have a bike.

2. **Emma and Matt walked to the park. They walked by the pond. They sat on the bench to rest. They slid on the slide. They played on the swings.**
   Where did the children sit to rest?

   (F) the pond

   (G) the bench

   (H) the slide

   (J) the swings

3. **It started to rain. Emma and Matt ran home. They played with Emma's cat. They went to Matt's house. They fed his hamster.**
   What did they play with at Emma's house?

   (A) a cat

   (B) a hamster

   (C) a dog

   (D) Emma's little brother

DIRECTIONS: Read each question. Choose the best answer.

4. **What word begins with the same sound as the picture?**

   (F) bat

   (G) pig

   (H) kite

   (J) sun

5. **What word begins with the same sound as *duck*?**

   (A) truck

   (B) bring

   (C) push

   (D) dance

6. **What word ends with the same sound as *get*?**

   (F) sat

   (G) tip

   (H) run

   (J) girl

7. **What word ends with the same sound as *rash*?**

   (A) with

   (B) loud

   (C) brush

   (D) sharp

GO

DIRECTIONS: Read each word. Look at the underlined part. Choose the word that has the same sound as the underlined part.

8. p**ie**
- (F) bake
- (G) pin
- (H) cup
- (J) ride

9. r**ai**n
- (A) name
- (B) time
- (C) tan
- (D) spin

10. m**ee**t
- (F) net
- (G) sock
- (H) bead
- (J) play

DIRECTIONS: Read each word. Choose the one that is a compound word.

11.
- (A) every
- (B) football
- (C) play
- (D) after

12.
- (F) asked
- (G) glasses
- (H) sailboat
- (J) eating

13.
- (A) sadly
- (B) furry
- (C) hopping
- (D) pen pal

DIRECTIONS: Read each sentence and the word choices. Choose the word that best completes each sentence.

14. The show was so great, we _____ .
- (F) clapped
- (G) swam
- (H) chewed
- (J) blinked

15. Dad drove to the _____ to buy some food.
- (A) store
- (B) road
- (C) home
- (D) car

16. I rode to the _____ to play ball.
- (F) room
- (G) mad
- (H) park
- (J) time

17. Jake is my _____. We have the same mom.
- (A) run
- (B) before
- (C) sunny
- (D) brother

18. Trey likes to _____. He always has a book in his hand.
- (F) blue
- (G) read
- (H) shirt
- (J) could

STOP

Name _____ Date _____

Building Vocabulary
Writing

DIRECTIONS: Look at the picture. Read the word choices. Choose the word that goes with the picture.

Examples:

A. (A) cap   (C) jacket
    (B) box   (D) bat

Answer: (A)

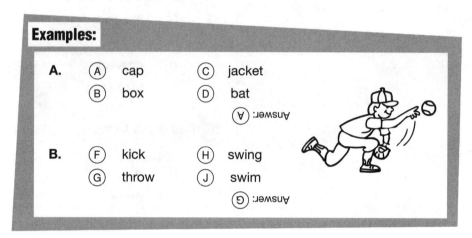

B. (F) kick   (H) swing
    (G) throw   (J) swim

Answer: (G)

1. (A) dance
   (B) run
   (C) sleep
   (D) read

2. (F) plate
   (G) coat
   (H) hat
   (J) blanket

3. (A) sledding
   (B) camping
   (C) shopping
   (D) running

4. (F) tent
   (G) car
   (H) van
   (J) bike

5. (A) one
   (B) two
   (C) three
   (D) four

6. (F) dog
   (G) girl
   (H) boy
   (J) cat

7. (A) winter
   (B) snowing
   (C) raining
   (D) summer

8. (F) sandcastle
   (G) toothpicks
   (H) jelly
   (J) rainy

GO

Name _____ Date _____

DIRECTIONS: Read the sentence and the word choices. Choose the word that best completes the sentence.

Example:

The phone _____ two times.

(A) ringing

(B) rang

(C) ringed

(D) runged

Answer: (B)

9. **My mother drinks _____ .**

(A) tea

(B) nails

(C) watermelon

(D) sandwiches

10. **The _____ on the radio was loud.**

(F) sun

(G) water

(H) music

(J) computer

11. **Lucy walked all the way to the _____ .**

(A) over

(B) cut

(C) jar

(D) park

12. **Maisie sat on the _____ .**

(F) touch

(G) something

(H) bench

(J) large

STOP

English Language Arts

4.0

Word Usage
Writing

DIRECTIONS: Read the sentence and the word choices. Choose the best words to fill in the blank.

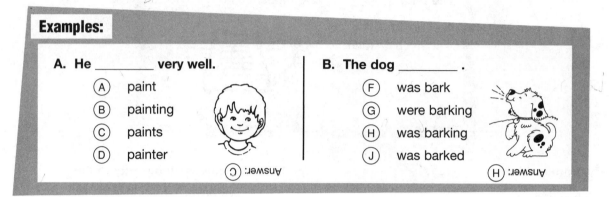

Examples:

A. He _____ very well.
- (A) paint
- (B) painting
- (C) paints
- (D) painter

Answer: C

B. The dog _____ .
- (F) was bark
- (G) were barking
- (H) was barking
- (J) was barked

Answer: H

 Clue Try each choice in the blank before choosing your answer.

1. **Harry is _____ this year than last year.**
   - (A) tall
   - (B) taller
   - (C) tallest
   - (D) most taller

2. **Jake and Winnie _____ .**
   - (F) swam together
   - (G) is a light
   - (H) faster than you
   - (J) fastest

3. **The fruit _____ juicy.**
   - (A) were
   - (B) am
   - (C) is
   - (D) will

4. **Her heart _____ fast.**
   - (F) was beated
   - (G) is beating
   - (H) is beat
   - (J) was beaten

5. **A caterpillar _____ leaves.**
   - (A) drink
   - (B) eated
   - (C) walks
   - (D) eats

6. **_____ to the store.**
   - (F) The corner
   - (G) They
   - (H) Anna
   - (J) We went

GO

DIRECTIONS: Read the sentence choices. Choose the sentence that is written correctly.

Examples:

C.
- (A) Them pies are good.
- (B) That boys are taller.
- (C) The cat purred.
- (D) They is nice.

Answer: (C)

D.
- (F) It is beautifulest.
- (G) We runned faster.
- (H) It was thundering.
- (J) He go home.

Answer: (H)

7.
- (A) Jacob leaved me behind.
- (B) I paid for the pen.
- (C) Can we went to the gym?
- (D) She walk fast.

8.
- (F) Last year, we wented to the game.
- (G) He will come last week.
- (H) Tomorrow was busy.
- (J) Today is a school day.

9.
- (A) Bob stand under the umbrella.
- (B) We sits on the bench.
- (C) The rain fell.
- (D) She are first.

10.
- (F) The sun rose.
- (G) Raccoons is friendly animals.
- (H) Deers isn't very big.
- (J) Mice likes cheese.

11.
- (A) The rabbit jumping high.
- (B) The new girl sit.
- (C) London is a city.
- (D) I goes to the park.

12.
- (F) She was so tires.
- (G) They eats lunch at noon.
- (H) The ice melting quickly.
- (J) Dinner was great.

STOP

English Language Arts

4.0

Synonyms
Writing

DIRECTIONS: Read the sentence and the word choices. Look at the underlined word. Choose the word that means about the same as the underlined word.

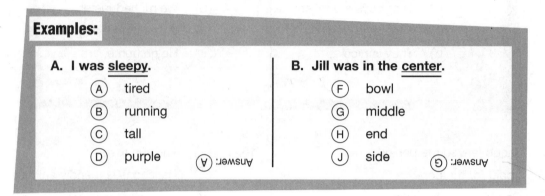

Examples:

A. I was <u>sleepy</u>.

   (A) tired

   (B) running

   (C) tall

   (D) purple   Answer: (A)

B. Jill was in the <u>center</u>.

   (F) bowl

   (G) middle

   (H) end

   (J) side   Answer: (G)

Clue   Think about what the sentence means before choosing the correct answer.

1. **The car was <u>speedy</u>.**

   (A) better

   (B) heavy

   (C) fast

   (D) able

2. **She is <u>lovely</u>.**

   (F) pretty

   (G) sharp

   (H) sad

   (J) near

3. **The soup is <u>steaming</u>.**

   (A) soft

   (B) spilling

   (C) hot

   (D) cold

4. **Kida <u>washes</u> the dishes.**

   (F) hides

   (G) cuts

   (H) sleeps

   (J) cleans

5. **It is a small <u>city</u>.**

   (A) house

   (B) bus

   (C) town

   (D) road

6. **We took a <u>boat</u> ride.**

   (F) car

   (G) balloon

   (H) ship

   (J) bike

STOP

English Language Arts

4.0

Antonyms
Writing

DIRECTIONS: Read the sentence and the word choices. Look at the underlined word. Choose the word that means the opposite.

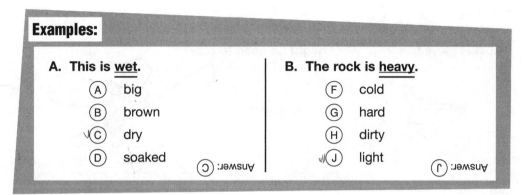

Examples:

A. This is <u>wet</u>.
- (A) big
- (B) brown
- ✓(C) dry
- (D) soaked

Answer: C

B. The rock is <u>heavy</u>.
- (F) cold
- (G) hard
- (H) dirty
- ✓(J) light

Answer: J

 Clue   Remember, the correct answer is the *opposite* of the underlined part.

1. The bear is <u>tame</u>.
- (A) black
- (B) wild
- (C) hungry
- (D) big

2. Susie <u>whispered</u> the secret.
- (F) yelled
- (G) tapped
- (H) cried
- (J) wrote

3. Why is it so <u>little</u>?
- (A) loud
- (B) bad
- (C) big
- (D) short

4. I run very <u>fast</u>.
- (F) slow
- (G) quick
- (H) around
- (J) loud

5. This is <u>easy</u>.
- (A) less
- (B) home
- (C) simple
- (D) hard

6. Jordan was <u>sick</u>.
- (F) ill
- (G) happy
- (H) well
- (J) tiny

STOP

English Language Arts

| 4.0/5.0 |

Matching Pictures With Text
Writing

DIRECTIONS: Read the story. Choose the picture that best answers the question.

Example:

Mikkel plays baseball. What might he need to play?

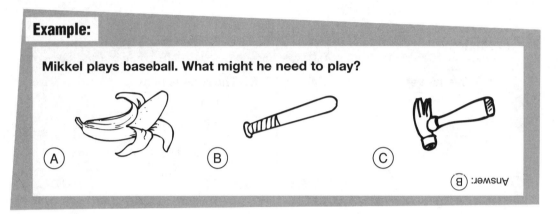

Ⓐ   Ⓑ   Ⓒ

Answer: B

 Clue   If you are not sure which answer is correct, take your best guess.

1. **Tomas loves to watch planes. He goes to the airport. What does he use to see the planes?**

   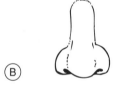   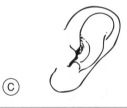

Ⓐ   Ⓑ   Ⓒ

2. **The weather is hot. What does Petra need to keep cool?**

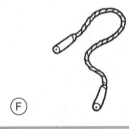      

Ⓕ   Ⓖ   Ⓗ

3. **Mark is going to the zoo. He wants to take some pictures. What will he take with him?**

Ⓐ   Ⓑ   Ⓒ

4. It was fun at the beach. The girls swam for hours. What did they wear?

 Ⓕ    Ⓖ    Ⓗ

5. Some animals are small. A mouse is small. Other animals are big. An elephant is big. Which of the following pictures shows the biggest animal?

 Ⓐ    Ⓑ    Ⓒ

6. We will visit Aunt Tina. She lives very far away. We want to get there fast. How should we travel?

 Ⓕ    Ⓖ    Ⓗ

7. Arthur built a clubhouse. It was in a tree. It was made of wood. He hung a sign. It said, "No girls can come in!" Who was upset about the sign?

 Ⓐ   Ⓑ    Ⓒ

STOP

English Language Arts

| 5.0 |

Changing Sentence Types
Writing

DIRECTIONS: Read the sentences and the answer choices. Think about how the sentence could be turned into a question that makes sense. Choose the best answer.

Examples:

A. I was very early.

- (A) Early very I was?
- (B) Was I very early?
- (C) I early very was?
- (D) Very I was early?

Answer: (B)

B. The horse is racing.

- (F) Racing is the horse?
- (G) The racing is horse?
- (H) Horse racing is the?
- (J) Is the horse racing?

Answer: (J)

 Clue   Say each answer choice to yourself.

1. Bert was in the play.

- (A) In the play was Bert?
- (B) Was the play in Bert?
- (C) Was Bert in the play?
- (D) The play was Bert in?

2. They will go skating.

- (F) Will they go skating?
- (G) Go skating will they?
- (H) Skating will they go?
- (J) Go will they skating?

3. My name is Conrad.

- (A) Conrad my name is?
- (B) My Conrad is name?
- (C) Name my Conrad is?
- (D) Is Conrad my name?

4. The flower was in bloom.

- (F) In bloom was the flower?
- (G) Was the flower in bloom?
- (H) The flower in bloom was?
- (J) Flower in the bloom was?

STOP

English Language Arts

5.0

Identifying Complete Sentences
Writing

DIRECTIONS: Read each group of words. Choose which group is a complete sentence.

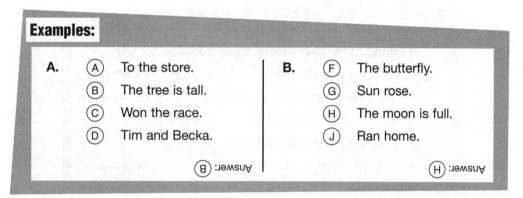

Examples:

A.			B.		
	Ⓐ	To the store.		Ⓕ	The butterfly.
	Ⓑ	The tree is tall.		Ⓖ	Sun rose.
	Ⓒ	Won the race.		Ⓗ	The moon is full.
	Ⓓ	Tim and Becka.		Ⓙ	Ran home.

Answer: Ⓑ   Answer: Ⓗ

 Clue   Say each answer choice to yourself.

1. Ⓐ Our yard.
    Ⓑ It rained all night.
    Ⓒ Jumped up.
    Ⓓ He and his brother.

2. Ⓕ Chip flew the kite high.
    Ⓖ Under the rock.
    Ⓗ Some people.
    Ⓙ Stood in line.

3. Ⓐ Phone number is.
    Ⓑ Bird nests.
    Ⓒ Paco has a new coat.
    Ⓓ Waved her hand.

4. Ⓕ When was the?
    Ⓖ Was open all day.
    Ⓗ He picked the biggest one.
    Ⓙ Sang a happy tune.

5. Ⓐ Read the.
    Ⓑ To the zoo.
    Ⓒ It snows in the winter.
    Ⓓ Made a birdhouse.

6. Ⓕ Up the stairs.
    Ⓖ Likes to sing.
    Ⓗ Fish and frogs.
    Ⓙ Babies like rattles.

STOP

English Language Arts

5.0

Completing Paragraphs
Writing

DIRECTIONS: A paragraph is a group of sentences that are all about the same idea. Read the groups of sentences and the answer choices. Choose the sentence that best completes the paragraph.

Example:

It rained hard. There were many puddles. _____

(A) Birds built nests.

(B) We splashed in the water.

(C) The sun was hot.

(D) He made a snowman.

Answer: B

 Clue   The correct answer fits best with the other sentences.

1. **Hanna sat down to read. She read for a long time.** _____

   (A) She finished the book.

   (B) It was her brother's dog.

   (C) The radio was loud.

   (D) She rode her bike.

2. **The family went on a trip. They were going far away.** _____

   (F) They went on skates.

   (G) They took an airplane.

   (H) Kim did not like the apple.

   (J) He ate lunch with them.

3. **It was so dark. I looked up at the sky.**

   _____

   (A) I ate a cookie.

   (B) The fire was warm.

   (C) The grass was cool.

   (D) I saw many stars.

4. **Vera is my sister. She is older than me.**

   _____

   (F) My dog is black.

   (G) Our cat purrs.

   (H) She is also taller than me.

   (J) Mom went to work.

STOP

Name _____ Date _____

English Language Arts

Spelling
Writing

DIRECTIONS: Look at each word carefully. Which word is spelled correctly? Choose the best answer.

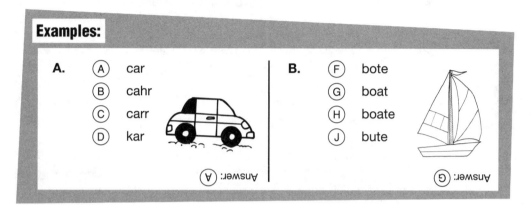

Examples:

A.
(A) car
(B) cahr
(C) carr
(D) kar

Answer: (A)

B.
(F) bote
(G) boat
(H) boate
(J) bute

Answer: (G)

Clue If you are not sure which answer is correct, take your best guess.

1.
(A) darc
(B) dahrk
(C) dark
(D) darck

2.
(F) furst
(G) first
(H) ferst
(J) forst

3.
(A) summer
(B) sumer
(C) sammer
(D) sumer

4.
(F) perty
(G) pritty
(H) pretey
(J) pretty

5.
(A) depe
(B) deep
(C) deap
(D) dep

6.
(F) papper
(G) paiper
(H) paper
(J) papr

GO

Name _____ Date _____

DIRECTIONS: Look at each group of words. Which word in each group is not spelled correctly?

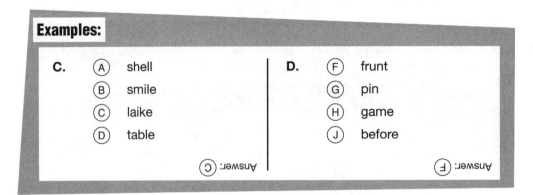

Examples:

C.   Ⓐ   shell   D.   Ⓕ   frunt

        Ⓑ   smile   Ⓖ   pin

        Ⓒ   laike   Ⓗ   game

        Ⓓ   table   Ⓙ   before

Answer: Ⓒ   Answer: Ⓕ

 Clue   If you are not sure which answer is correct, take your best guess.

7.   Ⓐ   brown   10.   Ⓕ   buzz

      Ⓑ   grean   Ⓖ   showd

      Ⓒ   white   Ⓗ   talk

      Ⓓ   black   Ⓙ   listen

8.   Ⓕ   therd   11.   Ⓐ   kite

      Ⓖ   second   Ⓑ   playing

      Ⓗ   first   Ⓒ   balloon

      Ⓙ   fourth   Ⓓ   cleen

9.   Ⓐ   park   12.   Ⓕ   house

      Ⓑ   bank   Ⓖ   school

      Ⓒ   trunck   Ⓗ   store

      Ⓓ   wheel   Ⓙ   mahl

STOP

English Language Arts

6.0

Capitalization
Writing

DIRECTIONS: Read each sentence. Which word in the sentence needs to be capitalized? If no more capital letters are needed, choose "none."

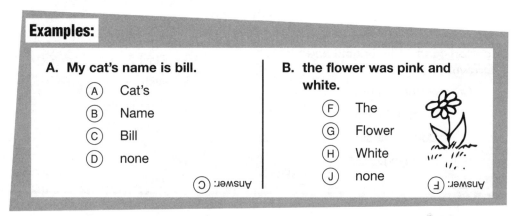

Examples:

A. My cat's name is bill.

- (A) Cat's
- (B) Name
- (C) Bill
- (D) none

Answer: (C)

B. the flower was pink and white.

- (F) The
- (G) Flower
- (H) White
- (J) none

Answer: (F)

Clue   All sentences begin with capital letters. Names and place names begin with a capital letter.

---

1. School starts at 8:30.
- (A) Starts
- (B) At
- (C) 8:30
- (D) none

2. Her sister lives in michigan.
- (F) Sister
- (G) Lives
- (H) Michigan
- (J) none

3. May i go to the park?
- (A) I
- (B) Go
- (C) Park
- (D) none

4. We went to the zoo on friday.
- (F) Went
- (G) On
- (H) Friday
- (J) none

GO

Name _____ Date _____

DIRECTIONS: Read each story. Look at the underlined part. Think about how it should be written. Choose the best answer.

DIRECTIONS: Read each sentence. Think about which word needs a capital letter. Choose the best answer. Practice with the example. Then answer numbers 7–9 the same way.

Examples:

C. **We got a new dog. We named her <u>cotton candy</u>. She is gold and brown.**

   (A)   cotton Candy

   (B)   Cotton Candy

   (C)   Cotton candy

   (D)   no change

Answer: (B)

D. **Jack played with tommy today.**

   (F)   Played

   (G)   With

   (H)   Tommy

   (J)   Today

Answer: (H)

The Race

We ran in a race. It was on
     (5)
<u>Saturday, april 10</u>. We went down
     (6)
<u>main Street</u>. Then, we turned on
Jackson Avenue. Timmy won!

5. **How should the day of the race be written?**

   (A)   Saturday, April 10

   (B)   saturday, April 10

   (C)   saturday, april 10

   (D)   no change

6. **How should the name of the first street be written?**

   (F)   Main street

   (G)   Main Street

   (H)   main street

   (J)   no change

7. **We start school on monday.**

   (A)   Start

   (B)   School

   (C)   Monday

   (D)   On

8. **we saw a bear.**

   (F)   We

   (G)   Saw

   (H)   Bear

   (J)   A

9. **She lives in washington now.**

   (A)   Lives

   (B)   In

   (C)   Washington

   (D)   Now

STOP

Name _____ Date _____

English Language Arts

Punctuation
Writing

DIRECTIONS: Read the sentences. Choose the correct punctuation mark for the end of the sentence. If none is needed, mark "none."

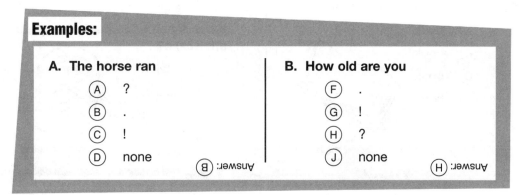

Examples:

A. The horse ran

- (A) ?
- (B) .
- (C) !
- (D) none

Answer: (B)

B. How old are you

- (F) .
- (G) !
- (H) ?
- (J) none

Answer: (H)

 Clue   Look for the missing mark at the end of the sentences.

1. I like peanut butter
- (A) .
- (B) ?
- (C) !
- (D) none

2. Can Tish come over
- (F) .
- (G) ?
- (H) !
- (J) none

3. That is so huge
- (A) ?
- (B) !
- (C) .
- (D) none

4. Harvey caught a fish
- (F) .
- (G) ?
- (H) !
- (J) none

5. May I have more
- (A) .
- (B) ?
- (C) !
- (D) none

6. That is amazing
- (F) !
- (G) ?
- (H) .
- (J) none

GO

DIRECTIONS: Read the sentence. Does it need a punctuation mark? Choose the correct punctuation.

DIRECTIONS: Read the sentences and the questions. Choose the correct answer.

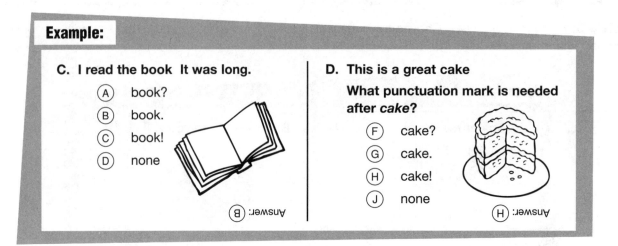

Example:

C. I read the book It was long.

- (A) book?
- (B) book.
- (C) book!
- (D) none

Answer: (B)

D. This is a great cake

What punctuation mark is needed after *cake*?

- (F) cake?
- (G) cake.
- (H) cake!
- (J) none

Answer: (H)

---

(7)
What is that I think it is a
(8)
mouse! I am not scared

7.
- (A) that.
- (B) that!
- (C) that?
- (D) none

8.
- (F) scared?
- (G) scared.
- (H) scared!
- (J) none

Time to Go

The party starts at two o'clock.
(9)
Oh, no We will be late. Where are your
(10)
shoes It is time to go.

9. **What punctuation mark is needed after "Oh, no"?**
- (A) no.
- (B) no?
- (C) no!
- (D) none

10. **What punctuation mark is needed after "shoes"?**
- (F) shoes?
- (G) shoes!
- (H) shoes.
- (J) none

STOP

English Language Arts

| 4.0–6.0 |

For pages 22–38

| **Mini-Test 2** |

Writing

DIRECTIONS: Look at the picture. Choose the sentence that matches the picture.

1.

- Ⓐ The sun is hot.
- Ⓑ My pen does not work.
- Ⓒ Tanika swims every day.
- Ⓓ I like to play in the park.

2.

- Ⓕ Lee gave him a car.
- Ⓖ My dad has a new watch.
- Ⓗ I see the truck.
- Ⓙ They read together.

DIRECTIONS: Read the sentence and the answer choices. Choose the word that best fills the blank.

3. **The _____ scored three points.**
- Ⓐ ball
- Ⓑ net
- Ⓒ team
- Ⓓ shoe

4. **The _____ tasted great!**
- Ⓕ cake
- Ⓖ car
- Ⓗ boat
- Ⓙ pencil

DIRECTIONS: Read the sentences. Choose the sentence that is written correctly.

5. Ⓐ They raking leaves.
   Ⓑ I loves her very much.
   Ⓒ Mine hair is black.
   Ⓓ Uncle Teddy is old.

6. Ⓕ The pictures is ripped.
   Ⓖ We are freezing!
   Ⓗ The apple fallen.
   Ⓙ I lives by Kim.

7. Ⓐ She go to the park.
   Ⓑ Can play at my house?
   Ⓒ I likes to eat pizza.
   Ⓓ You are very tall.

DIRECTIONS: Read the sentence. Think about how the sentence could be turned into a question that makes sense. Choose the best question.

8. **My soda is gone.**
- Ⓕ My soda gone is?
- Ⓖ Is my soda gone?
- Ⓗ Gone is my soda?
- Ⓙ Soda is my gone?

9. **Kate's kite was stuck.**
- Ⓐ Stuck was Kate's kite?
- Ⓑ Was stuck Kate's kite?
- Ⓒ Kate's stuck was kite?
- Ⓓ Was Kate's kite stuck?

GO

DIRECTIONS: Read each answer choice. Choose the one that is a complete sentence.

10. (F) He eats lots of.
     (G) Down the road.
     (H) We played for a.
     (J) James loves to swim.

11. (A) The tree lost its leaves.
     (B) In the closet.
     (C) A huge box.
     (D) Marco and Juan.

12. (F) Cleaned my room.
     (G) Raked the leaves.
     (H) I did my homework.
     (J) Played on the swings.

DIRECTIONS: Read the sentences and the answer choices. Choose the best sentence that goes with the paragraph.

13. **We do chores. I wash the dishes. _____**
     (A) The dog barks.
     (B) My dad likes apples.
     (C) My brother puts the dishes away.
     (D) I like pizza.

14. **Dad made popcorn. He burned it!**

     _____
     (F) Mom opened the window.
     (G) Sparky ran in circles.
     (H) Can we go now?
     (J) I said hello.

DIRECTIONS: Choose the sentence that has the correct punctuation and capitalization.

15. (A) You are nice
     (B) george has short hair.
     (C) Andy is my friend.
     (D) i ran around the bases.

16. (F) The Dog barked.
     (G) Where is Jamila?
     (H) Stop that yelling
     (J) My pool is Deep.

17. (A) Where do you live
     (B) We found a big rock.
     (C) marcus is good at soccer
     (D) My Cat is yellow.

DIRECTIONS: Choose the best answer.

18. **Which word is spelled correctly?**
     (F) girl
     (G) teech
     (H) hapy
     (J) thare

19. **Which word is spelled correctly?**
     (A) blu
     (B) becaus
     (C) com
     (D) brother

20. **Which word is not spelled correctly?**
     (F) boy
     (G) shurt
     (H) before
     (J) could

STOP

English Language Arts

| 7.0 |

Doing Research
Research

DIRECTIONS: Read each story. Choose the best answer for each question.

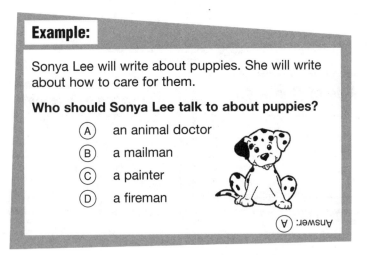

Example:

Sonya Lee will write about puppies. She will write about how to care for them.

Who should Sonya Lee talk to about puppies?

- Ⓐ an animal doctor
- Ⓑ a mailman
- Ⓒ a painter
- Ⓓ a fireman

Answer: (A)

Marnie wrote a story. It was about a trip. She went to a farm.

The farm had many animals. She milked a cow. She helped feed the pigs.

The farmer showed her the field. It had corn growing in it. Marnie picked an ear of corn.

1. Who did Marnie talk to about the farm?

- Ⓐ a teacher
- Ⓑ a farmer
- Ⓒ her brother
- Ⓓ a friend

2. Where else can she learn about farms?

- Ⓕ the library
- Ⓖ the car wash
- Ⓗ the park
- Ⓙ the grocery store

Anna wrote a story. It was about softball.

Her mom showed Anna how to hit a ball. She showed Anna how to catch a ball. She showed Anna how to run the bases.

Anna's story is about a girl who wins the game. The girl hits a home run. The girl is happy that she played so well.

3. Who did Anna talk to about softball?

- Ⓐ a dog
- Ⓑ a fireman
- Ⓒ her mother
- Ⓓ a teacher

4. Where else can she learn about softball?

- Ⓕ a music CD
- Ⓖ dance class
- Ⓗ gym class
- Ⓙ the zoo

STOP

English Language Arts

| 8.0 |

Using a Table of Contents
Research

DIRECTIONS: Read the table of contents. It tells the names of chapters and what pages they are on in the book. Use it to answer the questions.

Example:

Table of Contents

On which page will Maggie find information on oceans?

(A)   6

(B)   3

(C)   13

(D)   9

Answer: (C)

 Clue   Look at the table of contents before you answer the questions.

Shelly wrote a report. It is about animals in the zoo. Here is her table of contents. Use it to answer the questions.

Table of Contents

1. **Which chapter tells about fish?**

   (A)   2

   (B)   4

   (C)   3

   (D)   1

2. **What is the name of Chapter 3?**

   (F)   Snakes

   (G)   Fish

   (H)   Birds

   (J)   Tigers

3. **What is another chapter Shelly could add to her report?**

   (A)   Trucks

   (B)   Monkeys

   (C)   Pizza

   (D)   Doors

STOP

Name _____ Date _____

8.0

Using Resources
Research

DIRECTIONS: Read the words. Choose the word that comes first in ABC order.

DIRECTIONS: Read the question and the answer choices. Choose the best answer.

Examples:

A. **Which word comes first in ABC order?**

   (A) queen

   (B) bowl

   (C) pin

   (D) zoo

              Answer: (B)

B. **If you need the meaning of a word, you look in a _____ .**

   (F) map

   (G) dictionary

   (H) pencil

   (J) lake

              Answer: (G)

 Clue

Look at the first letter in each word to put them in the correct ABC order.

1. (A) flew
     (B) zip
     (C) hill
     (D) ant

2. (F) just
     (G) time
     (H) door
     (J) open

3. (A) head
     (B) yawn
     (C) line
     (D) new

4. (F) down
     (G) won
     (H) not
     (J) keep

5. **Danny is writing a report about soccer. Who could he talk to about it?**

   (A) his dentist

   (B) his brother

   (C) his coach

   (D) his mom

6. **Steve needs directions to a city. Where might he look?**

   (F) on a map

   (G) in a dictionary

   (H) in a newspaper

   (J) in a cookbook

7. **My report is about cooking. I talked to a _____ about it.**

   (A) police officer

   (B) chef

   (C) doctor

   (D) store clerk

STOP

English Language Arts

| 7.0–8.0 |

For pages 41–43

Mini-Test 3

Research

DIRECTIONS: For numbers 1–4, choose the word that comes first in ABC order.

1. (A) front
    (B) water
    (C) apple
    (D) before

2. (F) come
    (G) show
    (H) meet
    (J) when

3. (A) follow
    (B) three
    (C) bell
    (D) dance

4. (F) keep
    (G) leap
    (H) bird
    (J) stick

DIRECTIONS: Read the question. Choose the best answer.

5. **Tiffany needs to find out what a word means. Where should she look?**
    (A) in a dictionary
    (B) on a map
    (C) in a cookbook
    (D) in a newspaper

DIRECTIONS: Josh wrote a report about his dad's shoe store. He made a table of contents for his report. Look at the table of contents below. Use it to answer questions 6–8.

Table of Contents
Chapter 1—The Shoe Store. 2
Chapter 2—Kinds of Shoes 4
Chapter 3—Making Shoes. 8
Chapter 4—Selling Shoes 10

6. **Which chapter tells about making shoes?**
    (F) 1
    (G) 2
    (H) 3
    (J) 4

7. **Which chapter tells about the kinds of shoes his dad sells?**
    (A) 1
    (B) 2
    (C) 3
    (D) 4

8. **What is the title of Chapter 1?**
    (F) The Shoe Store
    (G) Kinds of Shoes
    (H) Making Shoes
    (J) Selling Shoes

STOP

Name _____ Date _____

English Language Arts

Understanding a Different Use of Language
Cultural and Social Language Use

DIRECTIONS: Read the story below about sign language. Then, answer the questions.

Sign Language

People who cannot hear or speak well use sign language. They use their hands to talk. Their hands make signals to show letters, words, and ideas.

Other people use sign language, too. Have you ever watched a sports game? Players use their hands to tell each other where to move. Have you ever been stuck in a traffic jam where there is a police officer? The police can use sign language to tell cars to go and to wait.

You also use sign language. You wave your hand when you say hello and good-bye. You use your fingers to point and show which way to go. We use our hands to make signals all of the time!

| A | B | C | D | E | F | G |

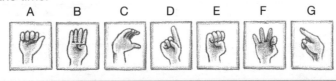

1. **Why do some people use sign language?**

   (A) They don't feel like talking.

   (B) They don't feel like listening.

   (C) They cannot ride a bike.

   (D) They cannot hear or speak well.

2. **What do people use to make signals?**

   (F) their hands and arms

   (G) their eyes, ears, and mouth

   (H) their feet and toes

   (J) their hair and head

3. **Who would be the most likely to use sign language?**

   (A) a boy playing at the park

   (B) a man who cannot hear

   (C) a woman who cannot walk

   (D) a girl learning to tie her shoe

4. **Why was this story written?**

   (F) to scare you

   (G) to make you giggle

   (H) to tell about sign language

   (J) to tell about sports

STOP

English Language Arts

| 11.0 |

Creating a Literacy Community
Cultural and Social Language Use

DIRECTIONS: Look for words around you at school and at home. What words do you see? Write down words you see every day that you can read on your own. Draw a picture of one of your words.

WORDS I SEE AT SCHOOL:

_____

_____

_____

_____

_____

_____

_____

WORDS I SEE AT HOME:

_____

_____

_____

_____

_____

_____

_____

Share your lists with one or two of your friends. Do you have any of the same words? Did you learn any new words?

English Language Arts

12.0

Exchanging Information
Cultural and Social Language Use

DIRECTIONS: Think of your favorite place. Where do you most like to go? Is it Grandma's house? Is it the library? Is it a place you went on vacation? Draw a picture of your special place. Then, write about it on the lines below. Share your special place with your friends.

_____

_____

_____

_____

_____

_____

STOP

Name _____   Date _____

English Language Arts

Mini-Test 4

For pages 45–47

Cultural and Social Language Use

DIRECTIONS: Read the story. Then, answer the questions.

Aidan's Walk

Aidan had to write a story for school. He did not know what to write about. He took a walk around town with his parents to think.

They stopped at the library. Aidan picked out a book about baseball. They walked to the video store. Aidan talked to the clerk about sports.

They then walked past the fire station. Aidan stopped to talk to Firefighter Tom. Tom used to play baseball when he was little.

Aidan and his parents walked past the store on their way home. They saw Mrs. Loo carrying a bag of groceries. Aidan helped her carry the bag.

Aidan talked to Mrs. Loo about his story. She thought he should write about baseball. Aidan liked that idea.

Aidan and his parents went home. He wrote a story about a baseball player named Tom.

1. **Who used to play baseball as a child?**

   (A) Mrs. Loo

   (B) the clerk

   (C) Firefighter Tom

   (D) the librarian

2. **Why did Aidan go on a walk?**

   (F) to think of a story

   (G) to play baseball

   (H) to rent a video

   (J) to borrow a book

3. **How did Aidan come up with an idea for his story?**

   (A) by reading a book about baseball

   (B) by talking to people around him

   (C) by playing baseball at the park

   (D) by watching a video about baseball

4. **While he was on his walk, where might Aidan have seen some new words?**

   (F) at the fire station

   (G) at the library

   (H) at the video store

   (J) Aidan might have seen new words at all of the places in the story.

How Am I Doing?

Mini-Test 1

Pages 20–21

Number Correct

15–18 answers correct	**Great Job!** Move on to the section test on page 51.
11–14 answers correct	**You're almost there!** But you still need a little practice. Review practice pages 7–19 before moving on to the section test on page 51.
0–10 answers correct	**Oops!** Time to review what you have learned and try again. Review the practice section on pages 7–19. Then, retake the test on pages 20–21. Now, move on to the section test on page 51.

Mini-Test 2

Pages 39–40

Number Correct

17–20 answers correct	**Awesome!** Move on to the section test on page 51.
12–16 answers correct	**You're almost there!** But you still need a little practice. Review practice pages 22–38 before moving on to the section test on page 51.
0–11 answers correct	**Oops!** Time to review what you have learned and try again. Review the practice section on pages 22–38. Then, retake the test on pages 39–40. Now, move on to the section test on page 51.

Mini-Test 3

Page 44

Number Correct

8 answers correct	**Great Job!** Move on to the section test on page 51.
4–7 answers correct	**You're almost there!** But you still need a little practice. Review practice pages 41–43 before moving on to the section test on page 51.
0–3 answers correct	**Oops!** Time to review what you have learned and try again. Review the practice section on pages 41–43. Then, retake the test on page 44. Now, move on to the section test on page 51.

How Am I Doing?

Mini-Test 4	4 answers correct	**Great Job!** Move on to the section test on page 51.
Page 48 **Number Correct**	3 answers correct	**You're almost there!** But you still need a little practice. Review practice pages 45–47 before moving on to the section test on page 51.
	0–2 answers correct	**Oops!** Time to review what you have learned and try again. Review the practice section on pages 45–47. Then, retake the test on page 48. Now, move on to the section test on page 51.

Name _____   Date _____

Final English Language Arts Test
for pages 7–48

DIRECTIONS: Read each question and the answer choices. Choose the best answer.

1. **Which letter begins the word *sunny*?**
   - (A) c
   - (B) s
   - (C) y
   - (D) l

2. **Which letter begins the word *bottle*?**
   - (F) d
   - (G) h
   - (H) b
   - (J) p

3. **Which word has the same ending sound as *slip*?**
   - (A) truck
   - (B) sash
   - (C) sunny
   - (D) map

4. **Which word has the same ending sound as *frog*?**
   - (F) gray
   - (G) tag
   - (H) begin
   - (J) mop

5. **Which word rhymes with *dance*?**
   - (A) make
   - (B) patch
   - (C) chance
   - (D) before

6. **Which word rhymes with *much*?**
   - (F) went
   - (G) tick
   - (H) touch
   - (J) rang

7. **Choose the answer that means the same or about the same as the underlined word.**

   I <u>like</u> eating watermelon.
   - (A) make
   - (B) enjoy
   - (C) hate
   - (D) pat

8. **Choose the answer that means the opposite of the underlined word.**

   The glass is <u>full</u>.
   - (F) empty
   - (G) broken
   - (H) mine
   - (J) hers

9. **Which word is not spelled correctly?**
   - (A) again
   - (B) could
   - (C) evry
   - (D) think

GO

10. Read the sentences. Choose the picture that matches the sentences.

This floats high. Some people ride them.

Ⓕ

Ⓖ

Ⓗ

Ⓙ

11. Choose the word that best completes the sentence.

The river _____ deep.

Ⓐ has

Ⓑ been

Ⓒ were

Ⓓ was

12. Choose the word that best completes the sentence.

The shelf _____ .

Ⓕ falling

Ⓖ falled

Ⓗ fell

Ⓙ flow

13. Choose the answer that is a complete sentence.

Ⓐ Now the group.

Ⓑ The middle part.

Ⓒ I ate the muffin.

Ⓓ The boy and his sister.

14. Choose the answer that is a complete sentence.

Ⓕ Ran down the street.

Ⓖ Brian was a.

Ⓗ The store on the corner.

Ⓙ We walked to school.

15. Choose the sentence that should come next.

Some food comes from animals. Milk comes from cows. _____

Ⓐ Eggs come from chickens.

Ⓑ Pumpkins grow fast.

Ⓒ Pigs like mud.

Ⓓ He walked the dog.

16. Choose the sentence that should come next.

The dish broke. There was a mess. _____

Ⓕ Jimmy was sleeping.

Ⓖ It was my birthday.

Ⓗ Mom helped me clean it up.

Ⓙ I found the book.

GO

17. **Choose the sentence that has the correct punctuation and capitalization.**

   Ⓐ honeybees live in hives.

   Ⓑ They make honey.

   Ⓒ have you ever been stung!

   Ⓓ It hurts?

18. **Choose the sentence that has the correct punctuation and capitalization.**

   Ⓕ I love winter Time.

   Ⓖ I like to Play in the snow

   Ⓗ I can make snow angels.

   Ⓙ i make great snowmen!

19. **Choose the word that comes first in ABC order.**

   Ⓐ butter

   Ⓑ water

   Ⓒ running

   Ⓓ cover

20. **Choose the word that comes first in ABC order.**

   Ⓕ head

   Ⓖ never

   Ⓗ grew

   Ⓙ open

21. **Josh needs to find out what a word means. Where should he look?**

   Ⓐ on a map

   Ⓑ in a dictionary

   Ⓒ in a newspaper

   Ⓓ in a cookbook

DIRECTIONS: Read the story. Then, answer the questions.

Rabbits are small animals. They have fluffy tails. Some rabbits have long ears so they can hear very well. Some rabbits have floppy ears. Others stick right up!

Rabbits eat all kinds of plants. They eat in fields. They eat in gardens. Some farmers do not like rabbits. They eat the vegetables the farmers grow.

Some people have pet rabbits. They keep them in pens or cages. Vegetables and grass are good foods for rabbits.

22. **What is this story mostly about?**

   Ⓕ plants rabbits eat

   Ⓖ farming

   Ⓗ vegetables

   Ⓙ rabbits

23. **Why do some farmers not like rabbits?**

   Ⓐ They run on the grass.

   Ⓑ They eat the vegetables the farmers grow.

   Ⓒ They make too much noise.

   Ⓓ They have fluffy tails.

24. **What are good foods for pet rabbits?**

   Ⓕ vegetables and grass

   Ⓖ hot dogs and candy

   Ⓗ vegetables and meat

   Ⓙ crackers and cheese

GO

Name _____   Date _____

DIRECTIONS: Look at the table of contents. Then, answer the questions.

Table of Contents

25. A table of contents shows _____ .

Ⓐ chapter names and pages

Ⓑ problems

Ⓒ what words mean

Ⓓ maps

26. Charlie wants to read about the fun house. Which page should he turn to?

Ⓕ page 5

Ⓖ page 7

Ⓗ page 10

Ⓙ page 14

27. Which chapter tells about roller coasters?

Ⓐ chapter 1

Ⓑ chapter 2

Ⓒ chapter 3

Ⓓ chapter 4

28. How many chapters are in this book?

Ⓕ 2

Ⓖ 3

Ⓗ 4

Ⓙ 5

DIRECTIONS: Read the story. Then, answer the questions.

The box was heavy. Simon needed help to move it. He asked Tom. He asked Kate. They went to help.

The box was full. It had books in it. Tom and Kate started looking at the books. They sat down to read. Simon sat down to read, too. The box stayed. They read their books for a long time. Then, they talked about their books.

29. How many people came to help Simon?

Ⓐ 1

Ⓑ 2

Ⓒ 3

Ⓓ 4

30. What did Tom and Kate do?

Ⓕ read the books

Ⓖ moved the box

Ⓗ ran away

Ⓙ ate some lunch

31. Why didn't they move the box?

Ⓐ It was purple.

Ⓑ They wanted to read.

Ⓒ Kate went home.

Ⓓ Simon told them not to.

32. What did the friends do after they were done reading?

Ⓕ They went to the park.

Ⓖ They went home.

Ⓗ They talked about their books.

Ⓙ They played a game.

STOP

Name _____   Date _____

English Language Arts Test
Answer Sheet

1 Ⓐ Ⓑ Ⓒ Ⓓ
2 Ⓕ Ⓖ Ⓗ Ⓙ
3 Ⓐ Ⓑ Ⓒ Ⓓ
4 Ⓕ Ⓖ Ⓗ Ⓙ
5 Ⓐ Ⓑ Ⓒ Ⓓ
6 Ⓕ Ⓖ Ⓗ Ⓙ
7 Ⓐ Ⓑ Ⓒ Ⓓ
8 Ⓕ Ⓖ Ⓗ Ⓙ
9 Ⓐ Ⓑ Ⓒ Ⓓ
10 Ⓕ Ⓖ Ⓗ Ⓙ

11 Ⓐ Ⓑ Ⓒ Ⓓ
12 Ⓕ Ⓖ Ⓗ Ⓙ
13 Ⓐ Ⓑ Ⓒ Ⓓ
14 Ⓕ Ⓖ Ⓗ Ⓙ
15 Ⓐ Ⓑ Ⓒ Ⓓ
16 Ⓕ Ⓖ Ⓗ Ⓙ
17 Ⓐ Ⓑ Ⓒ Ⓓ
18 Ⓕ Ⓖ Ⓗ Ⓙ
19 Ⓐ Ⓑ Ⓒ Ⓓ
20 Ⓕ Ⓖ Ⓗ Ⓙ

21 Ⓐ Ⓑ Ⓒ Ⓓ
22 Ⓕ Ⓖ Ⓗ Ⓙ
23 Ⓐ Ⓑ Ⓒ Ⓓ
24 Ⓕ Ⓖ Ⓗ Ⓙ
25 Ⓐ Ⓑ Ⓒ Ⓓ
26 Ⓕ Ⓖ Ⓗ Ⓙ
27 Ⓐ Ⓑ Ⓒ Ⓓ
28 Ⓕ Ⓖ Ⓗ Ⓙ
29 Ⓐ Ⓑ Ⓒ Ⓓ
30 Ⓕ Ⓖ Ⓗ Ⓙ

31 Ⓐ Ⓑ Ⓒ Ⓓ
32 Ⓕ Ⓖ Ⓗ Ⓙ

Mathematics Standards

Standard 1—Number and Operations *(See pages 58–68.)*
  A. Understand numbers, ways of representing numbers, relationships among numbers, and number systems.
  B. Understand meanings of operations and how they relate to one another.
  C. Compute fluently and make reasonable estimates.

Standard 2—Algebra *(See pages 69–73.)*
  A. Understand patterns, relations, and functions.
  B. Represent and analyze mathematical situations and structures using algebraic symbols.
  C. Use mathematical models to represent and understand quantitative relationships.
  D. Analyze change in various contexts.

What it means:
  ● Students should be able to model whole-number addition and subtraction situations using objects, pictures, and symbols.

Standard 3—Geometry *(See pages 76–80.)*
  A. Analyze characteristics and properties of two- and three-dimensional shapes and develop mathematical arguments about geometric relationships.
  B. Specify locations and describe spatial relationships using coordinate geometry and other representational systems.
  C. Apply transformations and use symmetry to analyze mathematical situations.
  D. Use visualization, spatial reasoning, and geometric modeling to solve problems.

What it means:
  ● Students should be able to identify shapes that have symmetry.

Standard 4—Measurement *(See pages 81–84.)*
  A. Understand measurable attributes of objects and the units, systems, and processes of measurement.
  B. Apply appropriate techniques, tools, and formulas to determine measurement.

What it means:
  ● Students should be able to measure length, volume, weight, area, and time, selecting appropriate units for what is being measured. Practicing with nonstandard as well as standard units will help students learn to apply appropriate measurement techniques.

Mathematics Standards

Standard 5—Data Analysis and Probability *(See pages 87–90.)*

    A. Formulate questions that can be addressed with data and collect, organize, and display relevant data to answer them.

    B. Select and use appropriate statistical methods to analyze data.

    C. Develop and evaluate inferences and predictions that are based on data.

    D. Understand and apply basic concepts of probability.

What it means:

- Students should be able to analyze data represented in simple graphs.
- Students should be able to determine outcomes of events as likely or unlikely.

Standard 6—Process *(See pages 91–96.)*

    A. Problem Solving

    B. Reasoning and Proof

    C. Communication

    D. Connections

    E. Representation

Mathematics

| 1.A |

Understanding Numbers
Number and Operations

DIRECTIONS: Look at the pictures. Read the question. Choose the best answer.

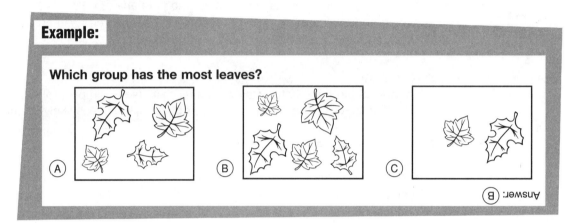

Example:

Which group has the most leaves?

Ⓐ   Ⓑ   Ⓒ

Answer: (B)

Clue   Look at all of the answer choices before you choose your answer.

1. **Which player is third from the left?**

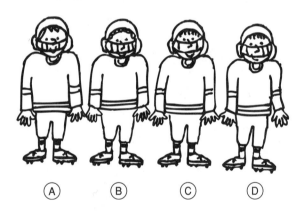

Ⓐ   Ⓑ   Ⓒ   Ⓓ

2. **Which basket has the most socks?**

Ⓕ   Ⓖ   Ⓗ

3. **Which numeral is thirty-two?**

Ⓐ   302
Ⓑ   5
Ⓒ   132
Ⓓ   32

4. **Count the bubbles. How many bubbles are there all together?**

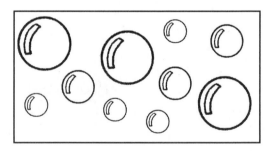

Ⓕ   9
Ⓖ   10
Ⓗ   11
Ⓙ   8

GO

5. How many blocks are there in all?

- (A) 26
- (B) 8
- (C) 46
- (D) 260

6. How many blocks are there in all?

- (F) two
- (G) seven
- (H) three
- (J) eleven

7. Which number shows 4 tens and 5 ones?

- (A) 405
- (B) 45
- (C) 9
- (D) 54

8. Which number shows 8 tens and 2 ones?

- (F) 8
- (G) 28
- (H) 82
- (J) 2

9. Which number is bigger than 63?

- (A) 56
- (B) 62
- (C) 59
- (D) 67

10. Which number is smaller than 71?

- (F) 70
- (G) 73
- (H) 84
- (J) 92

11. Which number means 20 + 4?

- (A) 42
- (B) 24
- (C) 20
- (D) 44

STOP

Mathematics

| 1.A |

Number Concepts
Number and Operations

DIRECTIONS: Look at the pictures and numbers. Read the question. Choose the best answer.

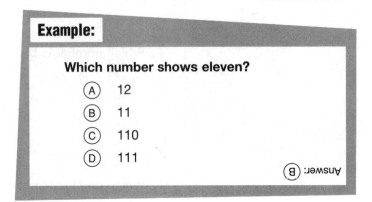

Example:

Which number shows eleven?

- (A) 12
- (B) 11
- (C) 110
- (D) 111

Answer: (B)

 Clue   Be sure the space you mark is for the answer you think is correct.

1. **Count the balls. How many are there?**
   - (A) 7
   - (B) 6
   - (C) 5
   - (D) 8

2. **How many dots are in the top part of the domino?**
   - (F) 4
   - (G) 5
   - (H) 9
   - (J) 10

3. **Look at the number in the box. Now look at the groups of apples. Which group of apples matches the number?**

- (A) 🍎 🍎 🍎 🍎 🍎
- (B) 🍎 🍎 🍎
- (C) 🍎 🍎 🍎 🍎 🍎 🍎 🍎
- (D) 🍎 🍎 🍎 🍎

STOP

Name _____ Date _____

4. Which number is the same as the word in the box?

- (F) 7
- (G) 55
- (H) 5
- (J) 15

5. Look at the number in the box. Which group of boxes is the same number?

- (A) ⬜⬜⬜⬜⬜⬜⬜⬜⬜⬜
- (B) ⬜⬜⬜⬜⬜
- (C) ⬜⬜⬜⬜⬜⬜
- (D) ⬜⬜⬜⬜⬜⬜⬜

6. There were 5 books. Two fell off the table. How many were left?

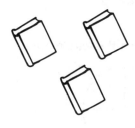

- (F) 5 + 2 = 3
- (G) 5 − 2 = 3
- (H) 2 − 3 = 5
- (J) 5 + 2 = 7

7. How many tens and ones are there in 31?

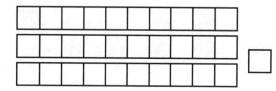

- (A) 3 tens and 1 one
- (B) 30 tens and 1 one
- (C) 1 ten and 30 ones
- (D) 10 tens and 3 ones

8. There are 3 flowers. Shelly planted 2 more. Which number sentence tells how many flowers there are in all?

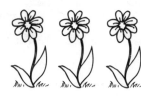

- (F) 3 − 2 = 1
- (G) 3 + 2 = 5
- (H) 3 + 5 = 8
- (J) 8 − 2 = 6

STOP

Spectrum Test Prep Grade 1

Mathematics 1.A

61

Name _____   Date _____

Mathematics
1.A

Number Relationships
Number and Operations

DIRECTIONS: Read each question. Look at every answer choice. Choose the best answer.

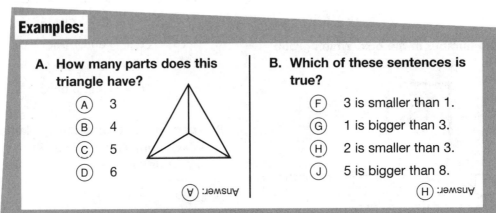

Examples:

A. How many parts does this triangle have?
- Ⓐ 3
- Ⓑ 4
- Ⓒ 5
- Ⓓ 6

Answer: Ⓐ

B. Which of these sentences is true?
- Ⓕ 3 is smaller than 1.
- Ⓖ 1 is bigger than 3.
- Ⓗ 2 is smaller than 3.
- Ⓙ 5 is bigger than 8.

Answer: Ⓗ

1. How many parts does this rectangle have?

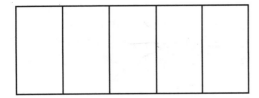

- Ⓐ 2
- Ⓑ 3
- Ⓒ 4
- Ⓓ 5

2. Which of these sentences is true?
- Ⓕ 9 is bigger than 11.
- Ⓖ 2 is smaller than 3.
- Ⓗ 4 is bigger than 5.
- Ⓙ 6 is smaller than 5.

3. Which of these sentences is true?
- Ⓐ 6 is smaller than 7.
- Ⓑ 10 is bigger than 11.
- Ⓒ 9 is smaller than 5.
- Ⓓ 8 is bigger than 9.

4. How many parts does this circle have?

- Ⓕ 2
- Ⓖ 3
- Ⓗ 4
- Ⓙ 5

GO

5. How many parts of this square are shaded?

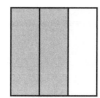

- (A) 0
- (B) 1
- (C) 2
- (D) 3

6. Which number comes fourth in this list?

2, 4, 6, 8, 10, 12, 14

- (F) 8
- (G) 2
- (H) 10
- (J) 14

7. How many parts of this rectangle are shaded?

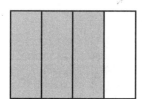

- (A) 1
- (B) 2
- (C) 3
- (D) 4

8. Which of these sentences is true?

- (F) 23 is smaller than 11.
- (G) 9 is bigger than 8.
- (H) 40 is smaller than 30.
- (J) 51 is bigger than 53.

9. How many parts of this circle are shaded?

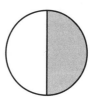

- (A) none
- (B) 1
- (C) 2
- (D) 4

10. Which number comes second in this list?

5, 10, 15, 20, 25, 30, 35

- (F) 5
- (G) 10
- (H) 15
- (J) 20

11. How many parts does this square have?

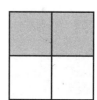

- (A) 1
- (B) 2
- (C) 3
- (D) 4

12. How many parts of the square above are shaded?

- (F) 1
- (G) 2
- (H) 3
- (J) 4

STOP

Mathematics

1.B/1.C

Addition
Number and Operations

DIRECTIONS: Solve each addition problem.

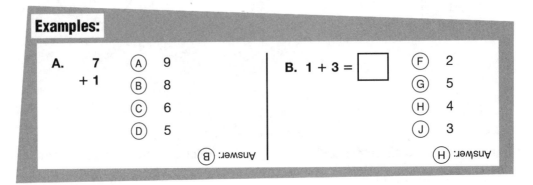

Examples:

A. 7
　　+ 1

- Ⓐ 9
- Ⓑ 8
- Ⓒ 6
- Ⓓ 5

Answer: Ⓑ

B. 1 + 3 = ☐

- Ⓕ 2
- Ⓖ 5
- Ⓗ 4
- Ⓙ 3

Answer: Ⓗ

 Clue   If a problem is too hard, skip it. Come back to it later if you have time.

1. 6
　　+ 2

- Ⓐ 5
- Ⓑ 11
- Ⓒ 8
- Ⓓ 4

2. 2
　　+ 8

- Ⓕ 10
- Ⓖ 6
- Ⓗ 28
- Ⓙ 16

3. 5 + 5 = ☐

- Ⓐ 5
- Ⓑ 55
- Ⓒ 10
- Ⓓ 0

4. 12 + 1 = ☐

- Ⓕ 4
- Ⓖ 11
- Ⓗ 22
- Ⓙ 13

GO →

5. $3 + 1 + 4 =$ ☐

- Ⓐ 8
- Ⓑ 0
- Ⓒ 13
- Ⓓ 7

6. $6 + 3 + 2 =$ ☐

- Ⓕ 65
- Ⓖ 11
- Ⓗ 5
- Ⓙ 10

7.
$$\begin{array}{r} 10 \\ 1 \\ +\ 2 \\ \hline \end{array}$$

- Ⓐ 103
- Ⓑ 7
- Ⓒ 12
- Ⓓ 13

8. $5 + 11 =$ ☐

- Ⓕ 15
- Ⓖ 16
- Ⓗ 17
- Ⓙ 6

9.
$$\begin{array}{r} 3 \\ 1 \\ +\ 5 \\ \hline \end{array}$$

- Ⓐ 16
- Ⓑ 10
- Ⓒ 2
- Ⓓ 9

10.
$$\begin{array}{r} 13 \\ +\ 5 \\ \hline \end{array}$$

- Ⓕ 8
- Ⓖ 65
- Ⓗ 18
- Ⓙ 15

11. $9 + 4 =$ ☐

- Ⓐ 5
- Ⓑ 12
- Ⓒ 13
- Ⓓ 16

12. $12 + 6 =$ ☐

- Ⓕ 14
- Ⓖ 6
- Ⓗ 16
- Ⓙ 18

STOP

Name _____   Date _____

Subtraction
Number and Operations

DIRECTIONS: Solve each subtraction problem.

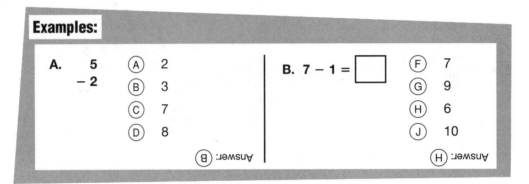

Examples:

A.   5   (A) 2
      − 2   (B) 3
            (C) 7
            (D) 8

Answer: (B)

B. 7 − 1 = ☐   (F) 7
                (G) 9
                (H) 6
                (J) 10

Answer: (H)

Clue   Get rid of the answer choices that are bigger than the numbers being subtracted. These cannot be correct.

1. 4 − 2 = ☐

(A) 2
(B) 6
(C) 24
(D) 1

2.   9
       − 4

(F) 13
(G) 12
(H) 5
(J) 4

3. 10 − 2 = ☐

(A) 8
(B) 12
(C) 10
(D) 6

4.   11
       − 9

(F) 20
(G) 2
(H) 10
(J) 19

GO

5. 6 − 1 = ☐

     Ⓐ 4
     Ⓑ 7
     Ⓒ 5
     Ⓓ 6

6. 12 − 2 = ☐

     Ⓕ 14
     Ⓖ 10
     Ⓗ 23
     Ⓙ 9

7.
$$\begin{array}{r} 9 \\ -\ 8 \\ \hline \end{array}$$

     Ⓐ 7
     Ⓑ 17
     Ⓒ 0
     Ⓓ 1

8. 9 − 9 = ☐

     Ⓕ 99
     Ⓖ 18
     Ⓗ 0
     Ⓙ 1

9.
$$\begin{array}{r} 8 \\ -\ 3 \\ \hline \end{array}$$

     Ⓐ 5
     Ⓑ 11
     Ⓒ 6
     Ⓓ 24

10.
$$\begin{array}{r} 13 \\ -\ 2 \\ \hline \end{array}$$

     Ⓕ 15
     Ⓖ 1
     Ⓗ 11
     Ⓙ 5

11. 12 − 4 = ☐

     Ⓐ 5
     Ⓑ 8
     Ⓒ 16
     Ⓓ 9

12. 21 − 10 = ☐

     Ⓕ 11
     Ⓖ 12
     Ⓗ 31
     Ⓙ 10

STOP

Name _____   Date _____

Mathematics

Solving Addition and Subtraction Problems
Number and Operations

DIRECTIONS: Read each question. Look at every answer choice. Choose the best answer.

1. Shawna's mom baked 8 big cookies. She gave 2 to Shawna. How many cookies are left?

    (A) 2
    (B) 6
    (C) 8
    (D) 4

2. Jake and Trey played soccer last night. Jake scored 2 goals and Trey scored 5 goals. Which number sentence shows how many goals they scored in all?

    (F) $5 - 2 = 3$
    (G) $2 + 3 = 5$
    (H) $2 + 5 = 7$
    (J) $5 - 3 = 2$

3. Becka bought a notebook at the school store for 60¢. She also bought a pencil for 15¢. How much did she spend in all?

    (A) 60¢
    (B) 15¢
    (C) 75¢
    (D) 85¢

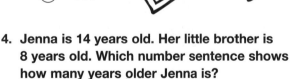

4. Jenna is 14 years old. Her little brother is 8 years old. Which number sentence shows how many years older Jenna is?

    (F) $8 + 14 = 22$
    (G) $14 - 8 = 6$
    (H) $6 + 8 = 14$
    (J) $6 + 6 = 12$

5. Oscar read 9 pages in his book. Paige read 12 pages in her book. How many pages did they read in all?

    (A) 12 pages
    (B) 15 pages
    (C) 20 pages
    (D) 21 pages

6. Last year, it took Chuli 27 seconds to run a lap in the gym. This year, he can run a lap 6 seconds faster than last year. How fast can Chuli run the lap this year?

    (F) 21 seconds
    (G) 24 seconds
    (H) 25 seconds
    (J) 27 seconds

7. Danielle weighed 45 pounds. Her baby sister weighed 14 pounds. Danielle estimated how much she and her sister weighed altogether. Which of the following is the closest estimate?

    (A) 40 pounds
    (B) 50 pounds
    (C) 60 pounds
    (D) 70 pounds

8. Marcos measured a pencil. It was 6 inches long. Marcos then measured a pen. It was 5 inches long. Which of the following is the closest estimate to the total length of the pencil and pen?

    (F) 5 inches
    (G) 10 inches
    (H) 15 inches
    (J) 20 inches

STOP

Name _____   Date _____

Mathematics

2.A

Identifying
Sequences and Patterns
Algebra

DIRECTIONS: Look at the pictures. Read the question. Choose the best answer for the question.

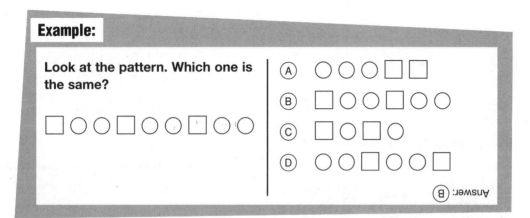

Example:

Look at the pattern. Which one is the same?

$\square \bigcirc \bigcirc \square \square \bigcirc \bigcirc \square \bigcirc \bigcirc$

Ⓐ $\bigcirc \bigcirc \bigcirc \square \square$

Ⓑ $\square \bigcirc \bigcirc \square \bigcirc \bigcirc$

Ⓒ $\square \bigcirc \square \bigcirc$

Ⓓ $\bigcirc \bigcirc \square \bigcirc \bigcirc \square$

Answer: B

 Clue   Sometimes, it helps to say the pattern to yourself before making a choice.

1. Look at the pattern below. Which group has the same pattern?

$\triangle \square \triangle \bigcirc \triangle \square \triangle \bigcirc \triangle \square \triangle \bigcirc$

Ⓐ $\triangle \square \triangle \bigcirc \triangle \square \triangle \bigcirc$

Ⓑ $\triangle \triangle \triangle \square \bigcirc \triangle \triangle \triangle$

Ⓒ $\square \bigcirc \square \bigcirc \square \bigcirc$

Ⓓ $\triangle \bigcirc \square \triangle \bigcirc \square \triangle \bigcirc \square$

2. Look at the pattern in the box. Which items will come next in the pattern?

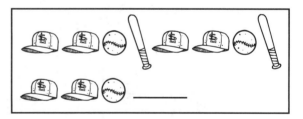

Ⓕ

Ⓖ

Ⓗ

Ⓙ

GO

3. Look at the number pattern in the box. If you count by twos, what number should be in the blank?

┌─────────────────────────────┐
│   │
│   2, ___, 6, 8, 10   │
│   │
└─────────────────────────────┘

(A) 7

(B) 4

(C) 12

(D) 11

4. Which picture shows the bears smallest to largest?

(F)

(G)

(H)

(J)

5. Count by ones. Which number comes after 15?

(A) 14

(B) 25

(C) 16

(D) 10

6. Which pattern needs the number 8 in the blank?

(F) 0, 1, 2, _____

(G) 2, 4, 6, _____

(H) 18, 28, 38, _____

(J) 3, 6, 9, _____

7. Count by twos. Which number comes after 12?

(A) 8

(B) 10

(C) 14

(D) 16

8. Which pattern needs the number 20 in the blank?

(F) 9, 10, 11, _____

(G) 12, 14, 16, _____

(H) 9, 12, 15, _____

(J) 5, 10, 15, _____

9. Look at the number pattern in the box. If you count by tens, what number should be in the blank?

┌──────────────────────────────┐
│   │
│   10, 20, ___, 40, 50   │
│   │
└──────────────────────────────┘

(A) 10

(B) 20

(C) 30

(D) 40

STOP

Name _____   Date _____

Mathematics

2.B

Understanding
Properties of Addition
Algebra

DIRECTIONS: Read the example. Then, choose the best answer to the problems.

> **Example:**
>
> When you add numbers, you can add them together in any order and get the same answer. Look at this number sentence:
>
>
>
> You can change the order of the first two numbers and still get the same answer. For example:
>
>
>
> So 2 birds plus 3 birds is the same as 3 birds plus 2 birds.

1. 9 + 11 is the same as _____ .

    (A)   20 + 8

    (B)   11 + 9

    (C)   14 + 6

    (D)   9 + 33

2. 2 + 5 is the same as _____ .

    (F)   5 + 2

    (G)   3 + 2

    (H)   1 + 2

    (J)   4 + 4

3. 6 + 8 is the same as _____ .

    (A)   8 + 2

    (B)   8 + 6

    (C)   7 + 6

    (D)   7 + 4

4. 7 + 2 is the same as _____ .

    (F)   5 + 2

    (G)   3 + 7

    (H)   2 + 7

    (J)   3 + 4

5. 4 + 5 is the same as _____ .

    (A)   4 + 8

    (B)   5 + 9

    (C)   4 + 6

    (D)   5 + 4

6. 8 + 9 is the same as _____ .

    (F)   9 + 8

    (G)   8 + 2

    (H)   9 + 7

    (J)   8 + 4

STOP

Mathematics

2.C

Using Mathematical Models
Algebra

DIRECTIONS: Read the example. Then, choose the best answer to the problems.

Example:

Sometimes, pictures can stand for numbers in number

sentences. In the number sentence below, 🍎 = 3

and ☆ = 1. What is the answer to this number sentence:

🍎 + 🍎 + ☆ = ?

Answer: 7

1. If ✏️ = 4 and ✂️ = 3, what is the answer for this number sentence?

✂️ + ✏️ = _____

(A) 5

(B) 6

(C) 7

(D) 8

2. If 🌞 = 2 and 🌼 = 5, what is the answer for this number sentence?

🌞 + 🌞 + 🌼 = _____

(F) 7

(G) 9

(H) 10

(J) 12

3. If 🐱 = 1 and 🐿️ = 6, what is the answer for this number sentence?

🐿️ + 🐱 = _____

(A) 6

(B) 7

(C) 8

(D) 5

4. If 🍎 = 7 and 🍇 = 3, what is the answer for this number sentence?

🍎 + 🍇 + 🍇 = _____

(F) 10

(G) 12

(H) 13

(J) 17

STOP

Mathematics

2.D

Describing Change
Algebra

DIRECTIONS: Read each problem. Choose the best answer that describes each change.

1. Sandy had a popsicle. She set it on the picnic table. The sun was shining. It got hotter and hotter. Which picture shows what happened to the popsicle?

 (A)   (B)    (C)

2. Dee was making a sand castle. She added a bucket of sand to it. She added another bucket of sand to it. Which picture shows what happened to the sand castle?

 (F)    (G)    (H)

3. In March, the puppy weighed 4 pounds. In April, the puppy weighed 7 pounds. Which picture shows how the puppy changed?

  (A)   (B)    (C)

STOP

Mathematics

1.0–2.0

For pages 58–73

┌─────────────────────────────┐
│   **Mini-Test 1**   │
└─────────────────────────────┘

Number and Operations; Algebra

DIRECTIONS: Read each question. Choose the best answer.

1. Which puppy is third from the bowl?

    Ⓐ   Ⓑ   Ⓒ   Ⓓ

2. Look at the number in the box. Which group of stars matches the number?

Ⓕ ☆☆☆☆

Ⓖ ☆☆☆☆☆

Ⓗ ☆☆☆

Ⓙ ☆☆☆☆☆☆

3.   How many tens and ones are there in forty-two?

Ⓐ 4 tens and 2 ones

Ⓑ 40 tens and 0 ones

Ⓒ 2 tens and 4 ones

Ⓓ 40 tens and 2 ones

4. Look at the blocks. Which number do they show?

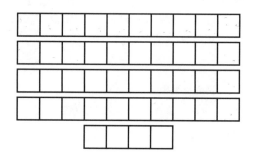

Ⓕ 404

Ⓖ 44

Ⓗ 80

Ⓙ 14

5. How many parts of this rectangle are shaded?

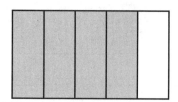

Ⓐ 2

Ⓑ 3

Ⓒ 4

Ⓓ 5

6. 3 + 2 + 4 = ☐

Ⓕ 11

Ⓖ 8

Ⓗ 7

Ⓙ 9

GO →

7.
```
   13
 −  4
```
  - (A) 8
  - (B) 9
  - (C) 10
  - (D) 11

8. Riley read his book for 12 minutes. Frank read his book for 7 minutes. What is the total number of minutes that they read?
  - (F) 5
  - (G) 12
  - (H) 16
  - (J) 19

9. Look at the pattern below. Which items come next in this pattern?

  - (A) ⬭ ▲
  - (B) ◇ ⬭
  - (C) ⬭ ◇
  - (D) ▲ ◇

10. 8 + 2 is the same as _____ .
  - (F) 2 + 7
  - (G) 8 + 3
  - (H) 2 + 8
  - (J) 8 + 10

11. If 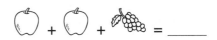 = 6 and ⬤ = 2, what is the answer for this number sentence?

🍎 + 🍎 + 🍇 = _____

  - (A) 12
  - (B) 14
  - (C) 8
  - (D) 10

12. Last year, Kyla was 45 inches tall. This year, she is 48 inches tall. Which picture shows how Kyla has changed?

  - (F)
  - (G)
  - (H)

STOP

Mathematics

3.A

Identifying
Attributes of Shapes
Geometry

DIRECTIONS: Read the problem. Look at the pictures. Choose the best answer for the question.

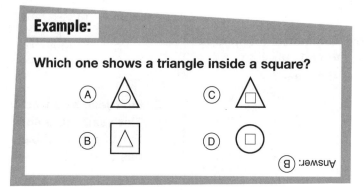

Example:

Which one shows a triangle inside a square?

Answer: (B)

 Clue   Use key words and pictures to help you find the correct answer.

1. **How many sides does a rectangle have?**

   (A)   3
   (B)   4
   (C)   5
   (D)   8

2. **Look at the triangle. How many sides does a triangle have?**

   (F)   3
   (G)   4
   (H)   5
   (J)   7

3. **Look at the shape. How many sides are there?**

   (A)   5
   (B)   8
   (C)   7
   (D)   4

4. **Look at the shapes in the box. How many circles do you count?**

   (F)   3
   (G)   5
   (H)   4
   (J)   6

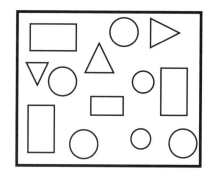

GO

5. Look at each group of shapes. Which one has the most stars?

(A)

(B)

(C)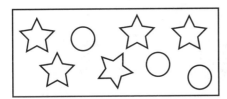

(D)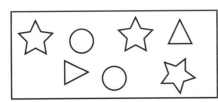

6. Which shape is *not* a triangle?

(F)

(G)

(H)

(J)

7. Which one shows a circle inside a triangle?

(A)

(B)

(C)

(D)

8. Look at the shapes inside the box. How many triangles do you count?

(F) 2
(G) 3
(H) 4
(J) 5

3.B

Identifying Positions
Geometry

DIRECTIONS: Look at the box of numbers. Use the numbers to choose the best answer to each question.

45	22	19	38
7	35	41	26
12	6	37	15

1. **Which of these numbers is above 37?**
   - (A) 38
   - (B) 35
   - (C) 26
   - (D) 41

2. **Which of these numbers is to the left of 22?**
   - (F) 45
   - (G) 6
   - (H) 15
   - (J) 26

3. **Which of these numbers is not near 15?**
   - (A) 37
   - (B) 7
   - (C) 26
   - (D) 41

4. **Which of these numbers is below 7?**
   - (F) 35
   - (G) 19
   - (H) 12
   - (J) 38

5. **Which of these numbers is near 6?**
   - (A) 37
   - (B) 19
   - (C) 38
   - (D) 26

6. **Which of these numbers is above 35?**
   - (F) 12
   - (G) 37
   - (H) 41
   - (J) 22

STOP

Spectrum Test Prep Grade 1

Mathematics

3.C

Symmetry
Geometry

DIRECTIONS: Read each question. Look at the pictures. Choose the best answer.

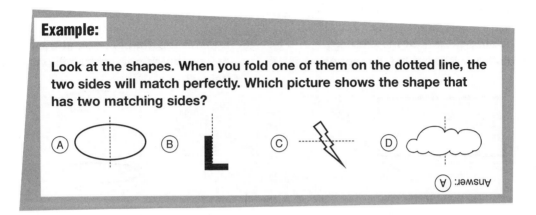

Example:

Look at the shapes. When you fold one of them on the dotted line, the two sides will match perfectly. Which picture shows the shape that has two matching sides?

Ⓐ   Ⓑ L   Ⓒ   Ⓓ

Answer: Ⓐ

1. Which picture shows the shape that has two matching sides?

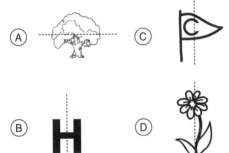

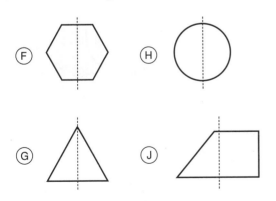

2. Which picture shows the shape that does not have two matching sides?

3. Which letter can be folded on the dotted line so the two sides match perfectly?

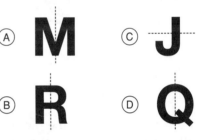

Ⓐ **M**   Ⓒ **J**

Ⓑ **R**   Ⓓ **Q**

4. Which picture shows the shape that does not have two matching sides?

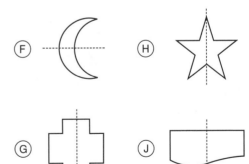

STOP

Name _____   Date _____

Recognizing Shapes in the Environment
Geometry

DIRECTIONS: Read each question. Choose the best answer.

1. **Look at the shape. Look at the pictures below. Which one is most like the shape below?**

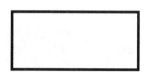

Ⓐ

Ⓑ

Ⓒ

2. **Look at the shape. Look at the pictures below. Which one is most like the shape below?**

Ⓕ

Ⓖ

Ⓗ

3. **Look at the shape. Look at the pictures below. Which one is most like that shape below?**

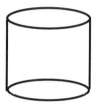

Ⓐ

Ⓑ

Ⓒ

4. **Look at the shape. Look at the pictures below. Which one is most like the shape below?**

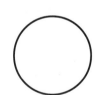

Ⓕ

Ⓖ

Ⓗ

STOP

Mathematics

4.A

Measurable Attributes
Measurement

DIRECTIONS: Read each question. Choose the best answer.

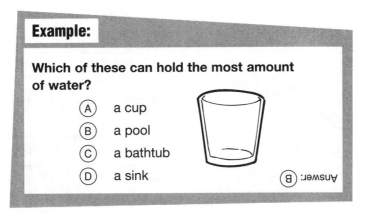

Example:

Which of these can hold the most amount of water?

(A) a cup
(B) a pool
(C) a bathtub
(D) a sink

Answer: (B)

Read the whole question and each choice before picking your answer.

1. **Which of these weighs the least?**

    (A) a book
    (B) a car
    (C) a boy
    (D) a balloon

2. **Which of these is the tallest?**

    (F) a building
    (G) a pencil
    (H) a chair
    (J) a room

3. **Which of these weighs the most?**

    (A) a baby
    (B) an elephant
    (C) a bed
    (D) a milk carton

4. **Which of these can hold the least amount of water?**

    (F) a car
    (G) a backpack
    (H) a spoon
    (J) a water bottle

5. **Which of these takes the longest amount of time?**

    (A) a day
    (B) a week
    (C) a month
    (D) a year

6. **Which of these is the shortest in length?**

    (F) a pair of scissors
    (G) a button
    (H) a ruler
    (J) a shoe

STOP

Name _____   Date _____

Measuring Time
Measurement

DIRECTIONS: Read each question. Choose the best answer.

1. **Look at the digital clocks. Which one shows the same time as the round clock face?**

Ⓐ 1:00   Ⓒ 2:00

Ⓑ 2:30   Ⓓ 12:00

2. **Look at the round clock faces. Which one shows the same time as the digital clock?**

4:30

Ⓕ   Ⓗ

Ⓖ   Ⓙ

Look at this part of a calendar. Use it to answer questions 3–5.

| | | | MAY | | | |
SUN	MON	TUE	WED	THU	FRI	SAT
1	2	3	4	5	6	7
8	9	10	11	12	13	14
15	16	17	18	19	20	21
22	23	24	25	26	27	28
29	30	31				

3. **What day of the week is May 3?**

Ⓐ Tuesday

Ⓑ Wednesday

Ⓒ Friday

Ⓓ Saturday

4. **How many days are in two weeks?**

Ⓕ 7

Ⓖ 5

Ⓗ 20

Ⓙ 14

5. **What is the date of the third Wednesday?**

Ⓐ May 8

Ⓑ May 18

Ⓒ May 31

Ⓓ May 26

STOP

Name _____ Date _____

Mathematics
4.B

Measuring Objects
Measurement

DIRECTIONS: Read the problems. Look at the pictures. Choose the best answer for the question.

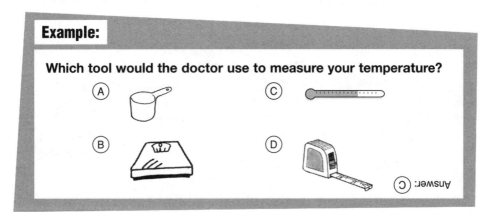

Example:

Which tool would the doctor use to measure your temperature?

Ⓐ   [measuring cup]

Ⓒ   [thermometer]

Ⓑ   [scale]

Ⓓ   [tape measure]

Answer: Ⓒ

 Clue Read the problem carefully. Then, choose the correct answer.

1. Look at the fish and the cat. Count how many fish long the cat is.

Ⓐ 2
Ⓑ 3
Ⓒ 4
Ⓓ 5

2. Look at the paper clips and the pencil. Count how many paper clips long the pencil is.

Ⓕ 2
Ⓖ 3
Ⓗ 4
Ⓙ 5

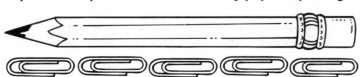

3. Look at the ruler. About how many inches is the marker?

Ⓐ 3
Ⓑ 4
Ⓒ 5
Ⓓ 6

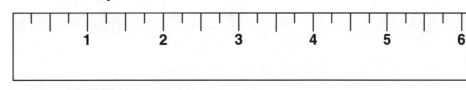

 GO

4. Look at the ruler. About how many inches long is the pair of scissors?

(F) 3

(G) 6

(H) 12

(J) 5

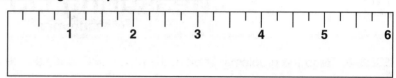

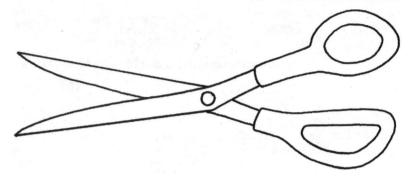

---

5. Jacob wants to weigh himself. He would use a _____ .

(A)

(B)

(C)

(D)

---

6. Peter is cooking. What will he use to measure flour?

(F)

(G)

(H)

(J)

---

7. Lydia can eat half a small pizza. Which picture shows how much pizza she can eat?

(A)

(B)

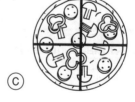
(C)

(D)

STOP

Name _____   Date _____

Mathematics

| 3.0–4.0 |

For pages 76–84

Geometry and Measurement

DIRECTIONS: Choose the best answer.

1. **How many sides does this shape have?**

   Ⓐ 4
   Ⓑ 5
   Ⓒ 6
   Ⓓ 8

   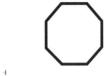

2. **Which one shows a square inside a circle?**

   Ⓕ

   Ⓖ

   Ⓗ

   Ⓙ

3. **Which sentence is true about these shapes?**

   Ⓐ The star is above the moon.
   Ⓑ The star is next to the moon.
   Ⓒ The star is below the moon.
   Ⓓ The star is on the moon.

4. **Look at the shapes. Which picture can be folded on the dotted line so the two sides match perfectly?**

   Ⓕ

   Ⓖ

   Ⓗ

   Ⓙ

5. **Look at the shape below. Which item below is most like that shape?**

   Ⓐ

   Ⓑ

   Ⓒ

   Ⓓ

   GO ⟹

6. **Which of these is the shortest amount of time?**

   - F   3 minutes
   - G   3 days
   - H   3 weeks
   - J   3 months

7. **Which of these can hold the most amount of water?**

   - A   a glass
   - B   a bathtub
   - C   a lake
   - D   a spoon

8. **How many days are in one week?**

   - F   2
   - G   7
   - H   4
   - J   8

9. **Look at the round clock faces. Which one shows the same time as the digital clock?**

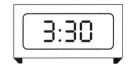

   A    C

   B 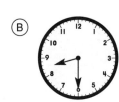   D

10. **Look at the ruler. About how many inches long is the pencil?**

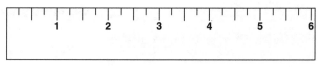

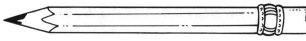

   - F   3
   - G   4
   - H   5
   - J   6

11. **Look at the fish and bear. Count how many fish long the bear is.**

   - A   6
   - B   3
   - C   4
   - D   2

12. **Dad is baking cookies. What will he use to measure the sugar?**

   F

   G

   H

   J

Mathematics

5.A

Representing Data
Data Analysis and Probability

DIRECTIONS: Look at the graph. It shows which toppings people like on their pizza. Use it to answer questions 1–4.

Favorite Pizza Toppings

✓ ✓ ✓ ✓ ✓	✓ ✓ ✓ ✓ ✓ ✓ ✓	✓ ✓ ✓ ✓	✓	✓ ✓ ✓

✓ = 1 Person

1. How many people like pepperoni?
   - (A) 6
   - (B) 5 ✓
   - (C) 12
   - (D) 3

2. What is the topping most people like?
   - (F)
   - (H)
   - (G)
   - (J)

3. How many people in all like cheese and pepperoni?
   - (A) 12
   - (B) 10
   - (C) 6
   - (D) 9

4. What topping is the least favorite?
   - (F)
   - (H)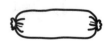
   - (G)
   - (J)

Mathematics

5.B

Analyzing Data
Data Analysis and Probability

DIRECTIONS: Look at the graph. It was made by Mrs. Park's class. It shows what pets the students have. Use it to answer questions 1–4.

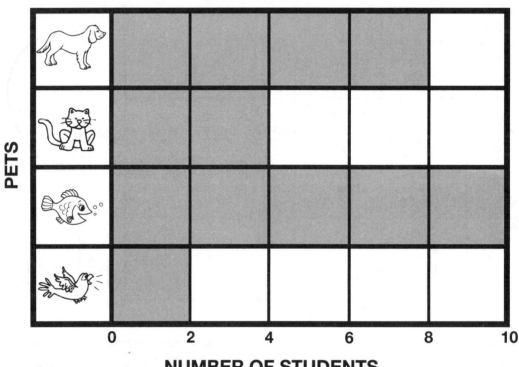

CLASSROOM PETS

PETS

NUMBER OF STUDENTS

1. Which pet do 10 students have?
   - (A) fish
   - (B) dog
   - (C) cat
   - (D) bird

2. How many students have cats?
   - (F) 8
   - (G) 5
   - (H) 4
   - (J) 6

3. Which pet is the least popular?
   - (A) cats
   - (B) fish
   - (C) birds
   - (D) dogs

4. How many more students have fish than cats?
   - (F) 2
   - (G) 6
   - (H) 10
   - (J) 12

GO

Name _____   Date _____

DIRECTIONS: Look at the chart. It shows which exercises are the most liked by the students in Mrs. Park's class. Use it to answer questions 5–8.

Exercise

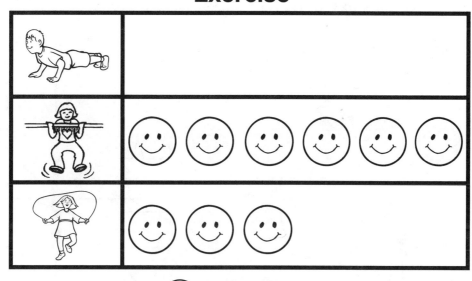

 = 1 Student

5. **How many students like push-ups?**
   - (A) 0
   - (B) 5
   - (C) 3
   - (D) 6

6. **Which exercise is liked the most?**
   - (F) pull-ups
   - (G) jump rope
   - (H) push-ups
   - (J) none

7. **How many students like both push-ups and pull-ups? Choose the number sentence that solves this problem.**
   - (A) $3 + 6 = 9$
   - (B) $3 + 0 = 3$
   - (C) $0 + 6 = 6$
   - (D) $3 + 5 = 8$

8. **How many more students like pull-ups than jumping rope? Choose the number sentence that solves this problem.**
   - (F) $6 - 5 = 1$
   - (G) $6 - 3 = 3$
   - (H) $6 + 5 = 11$
   - (J) $6 + 3 = 9$

STOP

Name _____ Date _____

Predictions and Probability
Data Analysis and Probability

DIRECTIONS: Read each question. Look at the spinner. Choose the best answer.

SPINNER 1

SPINNER 2

1. If you spin the arrow on Spinner 1, which shape is the arrow most likely to stop on?

   Ⓐ star

   Ⓑ heart

   Ⓒ square

   Ⓓ triangle

2. If you spin the arrow on Spinner 1, which shape is the arrow least likely to stop on?

   Ⓕ star

   Ⓖ heart

   Ⓗ square

   Ⓙ triangle

3. If you spin the arrow on Spinner 1, which shape will the arrow not stop on?

   Ⓐ star

   Ⓑ circle

   Ⓒ square

   Ⓓ triangle

4. If you spin the arrow on Spinner 2, which shape is the arrow most likely to stop on?

   Ⓕ star

   Ⓖ heart

   Ⓗ square

   Ⓙ circle

5. If you spin the arrow on Spinner 2, which shape is the arrow least likely to stop on?

   Ⓐ star

   Ⓑ heart

   Ⓒ square

   Ⓓ circle

6. If landing on a circle wins the game, which spinner would you want to use?

   Ⓕ Spinner 1

   Ⓖ Spinner 2

   Ⓗ Spinner 1 or Spinner 2

   Ⓙ neither spinner

STOP

Mathematics

6.A/6.B

Solving Problems
Process

DIRECTIONS: Read the story. Choose the best answer for each question.

Example:

Trista had 3 candies. Mom gave her 2 more. How many does Trista have now?

Answer: B

Clue Read the whole story. Look carefully at all of the answer choices.

1. Jim had 5 ants in his ant farm. He caught 2 more. Then, 3 ants crawled away. How many ants are left?

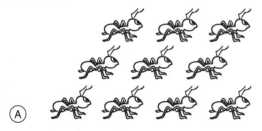

2. There were 8 cups of water. Yani drank 5 cups. Lonny spilled 2 cups. How many are left?

3. Boris ran 2 miles yesterday and 1 mile today. He will run 1 mile tomorrow. How many miles will Boris run in all?

(A) 2

(B) 4

(C) 6

4. Dean ate 9 apples. Then, he ate 3 more.
   Which number sentence shows how many
   apples he ate in all?

   (F) $9 + 3 = 12$
   (G) $9 - 3 = 6$
   (H) $9 - 6 = 3$
   (J) $6 + 3 = 9$

5. Jackie's dog had 6 puppies. How many dogs
   does Jackie have now?

   (A) $6 + 0 = 6$
   (B) $6 + 1 = 7$
   (C) $6 + 2 = 8$
   (D) $6 + 3 = 9$

6. I go to the movies. It costs $1.00 each time.
   I went Monday, Tuesday, and Saturday. How
   much did I spend in all?

   (F) $1.00 + $1.00 + $1.00 = $33.00
   (G) $1.00 + $1.00 + $1.00 = $3.00
   (H) $3.00 + $1.00 = $4.00
   (J) $1.00 + $1.00 = $2.00

7. The plant was 8 inches tall. Now, it is 13
   inches tall. Which number sentence shows
   how much the plant has grown?

   (A) $13 - 8 = 5$
   (B) $3 + 5 = 8$
   (C) $8 - 5 = 3$
   (D) $13 + 8 = 21$

8. Pepe lost 4 stickers this morning. He had
   8 stickers last night. How many are left?

   (F) $4 + 8 = 12$
   (G) $8 - 4 = 4$
   (H) $4 - 4 = 0$
   (J) $4 + 4 = 8$

9. Mihn ran the race. She won 1 ribbon. If she
   had 7 ribbons already, how many does she
   have now?

   (A) $8 + 1 = 9$
   (B) $7 - 1 = 8$
   (C) $1 + 7 = 10$
   (D) $7 + 1 = 8$

STOP

Name _____   Date _____

6.C/6.D

Using Mathematical Language
Process

DIRECTIONS: Read the problem. Look at the answer choices. Choose the best answer for the question.

Example:

Bobbie read 2 books. Howie read 3 books.
How many did they read in all?

Answer: C

---

1. The phone rang 3 times in the morning. It rang 6 times last night. How many times did it ring?

   Ⓐ $3 + 3 = 6$
   Ⓑ $3 + 6 = 9$
   Ⓒ $6 - 3 = 3$
   Ⓓ $9 - 6 = 3$

2. I raked 4 bags of leaves. Tyler raked 4 bags. Jess raked 2 bags. How many bags did we end up having?

   Ⓕ $4 + 4 + 2 = 6$
   Ⓖ $4 + 2 = 6$
   Ⓗ $4 + 4 + 2 = 10$
   Ⓙ $4 - 4 + 2 = 2$

3. Count each group of coins. Which group is worth the most?

   Ⓐ
   Ⓑ
   Ⓒ

   Ⓓ

4. Molly had 43¢. She lost 10¢. How much did she have left?

   Ⓕ 7¢
   Ⓖ 33¢
   Ⓗ 42¢
   Ⓙ 53¢

GO ➡

5. **Look at the digital clock. Which round clock shows the same time?**

 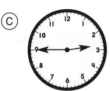

6. **Amy left at 7:00. Which clock shows the time she left?**

7. **Which of these sentences is true?**

Ⓐ A square has three sides.

Ⓑ One week lasts five days.

Ⓒ Four plus two equals twelve.

Ⓓ A rectangle has four sides.

8. **Look at the group of numbers. Which of these sentences is true?**

3, 6, 9, 12, 15, 18

Ⓕ The third number is 12.

Ⓖ The numbers go up by threes.

Ⓗ The last number is 15.

Ⓘ The numbers go up by twos.

9. **Look at the pattern. Which of these sentences is true?**

Ⓐ The pattern is circle, square, triangle.

Ⓑ The pattern is circle, triangle, square.

Ⓒ The next shape would be a circle.

Ⓓ The next shape would be a triangle.

10. **Dawn was 46 inches tall last year. She is 49 inches tall this year. Which of these sentences is true?**

Ⓕ Dawn is shorter than last year.

Ⓖ Dawn did not grow this year.

Ⓗ Dawn is 3 inches taller this year.

Ⓘ Dawn likes to swim.

STOP

Mathematics

6.E

Using Representations to Solve Problems

Process

DIRECTIONS: Read the problem. Look at the pictures. Choose the best answer for the question.

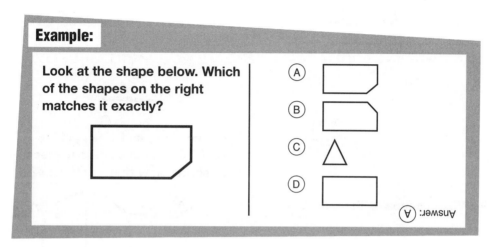

Example:

Look at the shape below. Which of the shapes on the right matches it exactly?

Answer: A

1. Look at the pictures. Which shows a rectangle with a triangle inside?

2. Look at these groups of shapes. Which group has 4 circles and 3 stars?

3. How many sides does an octagon have?

Ⓐ 4
Ⓑ 6
Ⓒ 8
Ⓓ 10

GO

4. Look at the ladder and the paper clips. How many paper clips long is the ladder?

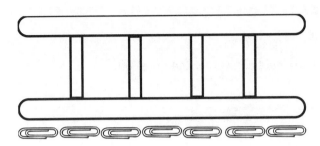

F 6
G 7
H 9
J 12

5. Use the ruler. Which animal is the tallest?

6. Which tool would a mother use to weigh a baby?

F    H

G 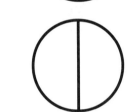   J

7. Tim, Tom, and Tina split a pie. They ate it all. Each got the same size piece. Which picture shows how they cut the pie?

A

B

C

D

STOP

Mathematics

5.0–6.0

For pages 87–96

Mini-Test 3

Data Analysis and Probability; Process

DIRECTIONS: Look at the graph. It shows how the students in Mr. Dell's class get to school. Use it to answer questions 1 and 2.

How We Get to School

Bus	☆☆☆☆☆
Car	☆☆☆
Bike	☆☆☆☆
Walk	☆☆☆☆☆

☆ = 1 student

1. How many students take a bus to school?
   - Ⓐ 5
   - Ⓑ 6
   - Ⓒ 4
   - Ⓓ 3

2. How many students walk to school?
   - Ⓕ 2
   - Ⓖ 3
   - Ⓗ 4
   - Ⓙ 5

DIRECTIONS: Look at the graph. It was made by Mrs. Kline's class. It shows what part of the zoo is the students' favorite. Use it to answer questions 3 and 4.

Favorite Part of Zoo	Number
Monkeys	✓✓✓
Penguins	✓✓✓✓
Tigers	✓✓✓
Giraffes	✓✓✓
Snakes	✓✓

✓ = 1 student

3. How many students liked the penguins the best at the zoo?
   - Ⓐ 2
   - Ⓑ 3
   - Ⓒ 4
   - Ⓓ 5

4. How many students in all liked the monkeys and the tigers?
   - Ⓕ 5
   - Ⓖ 7
   - Ⓗ 8
   - Ⓙ 9

GO

Name _____ Date _____

DIRECTIONS: Read each question. Choose the best answer.

5. **Which shape on this spinner is the arrow most likely to land on during a game?**

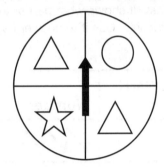

    Ⓐ   star

    Ⓑ   triangle

    Ⓒ   circle

    Ⓓ   heart

6. **Luke has 6 marbles. Mark has 12 marbles. Which number sentence shows how many they have in all?**

    Ⓕ $12 - 6 = 6$

    Ⓖ $6 - 6 = 0$

    Ⓗ $12 + 6 = 18$

    Ⓙ $12 + 4 = 16$

7. **Suzy had 39¢. She lost 25¢. How much did she have left?**

    Ⓐ   14¢

    Ⓑ   25¢

    Ⓒ   12¢

    Ⓓ   16¢

8. **Which of these sentences is true?**

    Ⓕ   A triangle has four sides.

    Ⓖ   Five plus two equals nine.

    Ⓗ   One week lasts three days.

    Ⓙ   A square has four sides.

9. **Amy has dance class at 5:00. Which clock shows this time?**

  Ⓐ    Ⓒ

  Ⓑ    Ⓓ

10. **Look at these groups of shapes. Which group has 4 stars and 3 circles?**

  Ⓕ

  Ⓖ

  Ⓗ

  Ⓙ

STOP

How Am I Doing?

Mini-Test 1

Pages 74–75

Number Correct

[ ]

10–12 answers correct	**Great Job!** Move on to the section test on page 100.
8–9 answers correct	**You're almost there!** But you still need a little practice. Review practice pages 58–73 before moving on to the section test on page 100.
0–7 answers correct	**Oops!** Time to review what you have learned and try again. Review the practice section on pages 58–73. Then, retake the test on page 74–75. Now, move on to the section test on page 100.

Mini-Test 2

Pages 85–86

Number Correct

[ ]

10–12 answers correct	**Awesome!** Move on to the section test on page 100.
8–9 answers correct	**You're almost there!** But you still need a little practice. Review practice pages 76–84 before moving on to the section test on page 100.
0–7 answers correct	**Oops!** Time to review what you have learned and try again. Review the practice section on pages 76–84. Then, retake the test on page 85–86. Now, move on to the section test on page 100.

Mini-Test 3

Pages 97–98

Number Correct

[ ]

9–10 answers correct	**Great Job!** Move on to the section test on page 100.
6–8 answers correct	**You're almost there!** But you still need a little practice. Review practice pages 87–96 before moving on to the section test on page 100.
0–5 answers correct	**Oops!** Time to review what you have learned and try again. Review the practice section on pages 87–96. Then, retake the test on page 97–98. Now, move on to the section test on page 100.

Final Mathematics Test
for pages 58–98

DIRECTIONS: Choose the best answer.

1. How many stars are in this group?

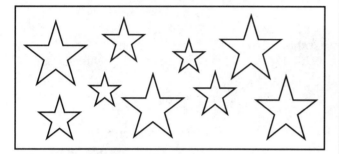

- (A) 7
- (B) 8
- (C) 9
- (D) 10

2. Which plant is the tallest?

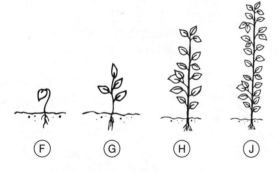

- (F)   (G)   (H)   (J)

3. Look at the pattern. Which shape should be next?

- (A) circle
- (B) square
- (C) star
- (D) triangle

4. Look at the pattern. Which number should be next?

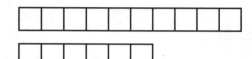

2, 4, 6, ___, 10, 12

- (F) 14
- (G) 8
- (H) 9
- (J) 7

5. What number is shown here?

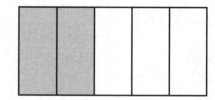

- (A) 70
- (B) 16
- (C) 7
- (D) 12

6. Which number is fifty-seven?

- (F) 27
- (G) 57
- (H) 47
- (J) 7

7. How many parts of this rectangle are shaded?

- (A) 2
- (B) 3
- (C) 4
- (D) 5

GO

8. Which number comes third in this list?

5, 10, 15, 20, 25, 30

(F) 25

(G) 30

(H) 15

(J) 40

9.　　12
　　　+ 5

(A) 17

(B) 13

(C) 7

(D) 16

10. 22 − 8 = ☐

(F) 16

(G) 6

(H) 4

(J) 14

11. Ramon scored 14 points in his first game and 9 points in his second game. Which number sentence shows how many points he scored in all?

(A) 14 − 9 = 5

(B) 14 + 9 = 23

(C) 9 + 9 = 18

(D) 9 + 3 = 12

12. 2 + 5 is the same as _____ .

(F) 2 + 3

(G) 8 + 4

(H) 5 + 2

(J) 5 − 2

13. If  = 4 and = 3, which is the answer for this number sentence?

 + + = _____

(A) 7

(B) 10

(C) 11

(D) 14

14. Last month, the baby weighed 7 pounds. This month, the baby weighs 11 pounds. Which of these sentences is true?

(F) The baby lost 3 pounds.

(G) The baby gained 4 pounds.

(H) The baby lost 2 pounds.

(J) The baby gained 6 pounds.

15. How many sides does this shape have?

(A) 3

(B) 4

(C) 5

(D) 6

16. Which one shows a square inside a circle?

(F)

(G)

(H)

(J)

GO

Name _____   Date _____

17. Which picture can be folded on the dotted line so the two sides match perfectly?

Ⓐ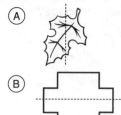

Ⓑ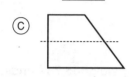

Ⓒ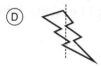

Ⓓ

18. Which of these takes the longest amount of time?

Ⓕ recess

Ⓖ a school day

Ⓗ a week

Ⓙ summer

19. Which of these can hold the least?

Ⓐ a pool

Ⓑ a lake

Ⓒ a glass

Ⓓ a sink

20. About how many paper clips long is this spoon?

Ⓕ 5

Ⓖ 6

Ⓗ 4

Ⓙ 3

DIRECTIONS: Use this graph to answer questions 21–23.

Birthdays

January	☆ ☆ ☆ ☆ ☆
February	☆ ☆ ☆
March	☆ ☆ ☆ ☆
April	☆
May	☆ ☆ ☆
June	☆ ☆

☆ = 1 student

21. How many students have birthdays in March?

Ⓐ 5

Ⓑ 2

Ⓒ 4

Ⓓ 3

22. Which month has the smallest number of birthdays?

Ⓕ April

Ⓖ June

Ⓗ May

Ⓙ January

23. How many students in all are in this class?

Ⓐ 15

Ⓑ 17

Ⓒ 13

Ⓓ 18

GO

Name _____   Date _____

DIRECTIONS: Choose the best answer.

24. Which shape is most likely to come up on this spinner?

- (F) circle
- (G) triangle
- (H) square
- (J) star

25. Nikki read 4 books. Rachel read 6 books. How many books did they read in all?

- (A) $4 + 4 = 8$
- (B) $6 - 4 = 2$
- (C) $4 + 6 = 10$
- (D) $6 - 6 = 0$

26. Which of these sentences is true?

- (F) A rectangle has three sides.
- (G) Six plus three equals nine.
- (H) A circle has four sides.
- (J) One plus four equals seven.

27. Kate and Nina split a pizza. Each got the same size piece. Which picture shows how they cut the pizza?

- (A)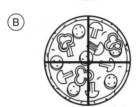
- (B)
- (C)
- (D)

28. Look at the digital clock. Which round clock shows the same time?

- (F)
- (H)
- (G)
- (J)

STOP

Name _____   Date _____

Final Mathematics Test
Answer Sheet

1 (A) (B) (C) (D)
2 (F) (G) (H) (J)
3 (A) (B) (C) (D)
4 (F) (G) (H) (J)
5 (A) (B) (C) (D)
6 (F) (G) (H) (J)
7 (A) (B) (C) (D)
8 (F) (G) (H) (J)
9 (A) (B) (C) (D)
10 (F) (G) (H) (J)

11 (A) (B) (C) (D)
12 (F) (G) (H) (J)
13 (A) (B) (C) (D)
14 (F) (G) (H) (J)
15 (A) (B) (C) (D)
16 (F) (G) (H) (J)
17 (A) (B) (C) (D)
18 (F) (G) (H) (J)
19 (A) (B) (C) (D)
20 (F) (G) (H) (J)

21 (A) (B) (C) (D)
22 (F) (G) (H) (J)
23 (A) (B) (C) (D)
24 (F) (G) (H) (J)
25 (A) (B) (C) (D)
26 (F) (G) (H) (J)
27 (A) (B) (C) (D)
28 (F) (G) (H) (J)

Answer Key

Pages 7–8
1. B
2. F
3. D
4. F
5. B
6. J
7. C
8. G

Pages 9–10
1. B
2. F
3. D
4. F
5. C
6. G
7. A
8. J

Page 11
1. A
2. H
3. B
4. H

Page 12
1. D
2. F
3. B
4. H

Page 13
1. C
2. G
3. D
4. G

Page 14
1. D
2. F
3. C
4. J

Page 15
1. C
2. F
3. D
4. H
5. B
6. F

Page 16
1. D
2. F
3. B
4. H

Page 17
1. A
2. G
3. C
4. G
5. D
6. F
7. C
8. J

Page 18
1. C
2. H
3. C
4. F
5. A
6. H

Page 19
1. B
2. H
3. D
4. F

Pages 20–21
Mini-Test 1
1. C
2. G
3. A
4. G
5. D
6. F
7. C
8. J
9. A
10. H
11. B
12. H
13. D
14. F
15. A
16. H
17. D
18. G

Pages 22–23
1. C
2. J
3. B
4. F
5. A
6. G
7. D
8. F
9. A
10. H
11. D
12. H

Pages 24–25
1. B
2. F
3. C
4. G
5. D
6. J
7. B
8. J
9. C
10. F
11. C
12. J

Page 26
1. C
2. F
3. C
4. J
5. C
6. H

Page 27
1. B
2. F
3. C
4. F
5. D
6. H

Pages 28–29
1. A
2. G
3. B
4. F
5. C
6. H
7. B

Page 30
1. C
2. F
3. D
4. G

Page 31
1. B
2. F
3. C
4. H
5. C
6. J

Page 32
1. A
2. G
3. D
4. H

Pages 33–34
1. C
2. G
3. A
4. J
5. B
6. H
7. B
8. F
9. C
10. G
11. D
12. J

Pages 35–36
1. D
2. H
3. A
4. H
5. A
6. G
7. C
8. F
9. C

Pages 37–38
1. A
2. G
3. B
4. F
5. B
6. F
7. C
8. G
9. C
10. F

Pages 39–40
Mini-Test 2
1. C
2. G
3. C
4. F
5. D
6. G
7. D
8. G
9. D
10. J
11. A
12. H
13. C
14. F
15. C
16. G
17. B
18. F
19. D
20. G

Page 41
1. B
2. F
3. C
4. H

Page 42
1. A
2. H
3. B

Page 43
1. D
2. H
3. A
4. F
5. C
6. F
7. B

Page 44 Mini-Test 3
1. C
2. F
3. C
4. H
5. A
6. H
7. B
8. F

Page 45
1. D
2. F
3. B
4. H

Page 46
Students should list
words they find both at
school and at home.

Page 47
Students should draw
a picture of a place
that is special to them
and then write about it.

Page 48 Mini-Test 4
1. C
2. F
3. B
4. J

Pages 51–54 Final
English Language
Arts Test
1. B
2. H
3. D
4. G
5. C
6. H
7. B
8. F
9. C
10. G
11. D
12. H
13. C
14. J
15. A
16. H
17. B
18. H
19. A

20. H
21. B
22. J
23. B
24. F
25. A
26. G
27. A
28. J
29. B
30. F
31. B
32. H

Pages 58–59
1. C
2. G
3. D
4. G
5. A
6. J
7. B
8. H
9. D
10. F
11. B

Pages 60–61
1. B
2. G
3. C
4. H
5. D
6. G
7. A
8. G

Pages 62–63
1. D
2. G
3. A
4. H
5. C
6. F
7. C
8. G
9. B
10. G
11. D
12. G

Pages 64–65
1. C
2. F
3. C
4. J
5. A
6. G

7. D
8. G
9. D
10. H
11. C
12. J

Pages 66–67
1. A
2. H
3. A
4. G
5. C
6. G
7. D
8. H
9. A
10. H
11. B
12. F

Page 68
1. B
2. H
3. C
4. G
5. D
6. F
7. C
8. G

Pages 69–70
1. A
2. J
3. B
4. H
5. C
6. G
7. C
8. J
9. C

Page 71
1. B
2. F
3. B
4. H
5. D
6. F

Page 72
1. C
2. G
3. B
4. H

Page 73
1. B
2. G

3. C

Pages 74–75
Mini-Test 1
1. C
2. G
3. A
4. G
5. C
6. J
7. B
8. J
9. C
10. H
11. B
12. H

Pages 76–77
1. B
2. F
3. B
4. J
5. C
6. F
7. D
8. J

Page 78
1. D
2. F
3. B
4. H
5. A
6. J

Page 79
1. B
2. J
3. A
4. J

Page 80
1. B
2. F
3. B
4. G

Page 81
1. D
2. F
3. B
4. H
5. D
6. G

Page 82
1. C
2. G
3. A
4. J
5. B

Pages 83–84
1. B
2. J
3. C
4. G
5. C
6. J
7. A

Pages 85–86
Mini-Test 2
1. D
2. G
3. B
4. F
5. B
6. F
7. C
8. G
9. D
10. J
11. C
12. G

Page 87
1. B
2. G
3. A
4. F

Pages 88–89
1. A
2. H
3. C
4. G
5. A
6. F
7. C
8. G

Page 90
1. A
2. H
3. B
4. H
5. D
6. G

Pages 91–92
1. C
2. G
3. B
4. F
5. B
6. G
7. A
8. G
9. D

Pages 93–94
1. B
2. H
3. D
4. G
5. C
6. H
7. D
8. G
9. A
10. H

Pages 95–96
1. A
2. J
3. C
4. G
5. B
6. G
7. C

Pages 97–98
Mini-Test 3
1. B
2. J
3. D
4. G
5. B
6. H
7. A
8. J
9. C
10. G

Pages 100–103 Final Mathematics Test
1. C
2. J
3. B
4. G
5. B
6. G
7. A
8. H
9. A
10. J
11. B
12. H
13. C
14. G
15. C
16. H
17. B
18. J
19. C
20. F
21. C
22. F
23. D
24. J
25. C
26. G
27. A
28. H

NOTES

NOTES

NOTES

NOTES

NOTES